Peace Ministry

A Handbook for Local Churches

Daniel L. Buttry

Judson Press ® Valley Forge

Peace Ministry: A Handbook for Local Churches
© 1995
Judson Press, Valley Forge, PA 19482-0851

Unless otherwise indicated, Bible quotations in this volume are from the New Revised Standard Version of the Bible, copyrighted 1989 by the Division of Christian Education of the National Council of the Churches of Christ in the United States of America, and are used by permission.

Other quotations are from *The Holy Bible*, King James Version. Revised Standard Version of the Bible, copyright © 1946, 1952, 1971, by the Division of Christian Education of the National Council of the Churches of Christ in the USA. Used by permission.

Library of Congress Cataloging-in-Publication Data
Buttry, Daniel.
Peace ministry: a handbook for local churches / by Daniel L. Buttry.
p. cm.
Includes bibliographical references.
ISBN 0-8170-1214-1 (pbk.: alk. paper)
1. Reconciliation—Religious aspects—Christianity. 2. Peace—Religious aspects—Christianity. 3. Violence—Religious aspects—Christianity. 4. Christianity and justice. 5. Peace movements—United States. I. Title.
BV4509.5.B88 1994
261.8'73—dc20
94-42198

Printed in the U.S.A.
95 96 97 98 99 00 01 02   8 7 6 5 4 3 2 1

Dedicated to

faithful peacemaking pastors:

*Steve and Mary, George, Gail, Nancy, Paul,
Dick, Tim, Lucius, Steve, Bruce, Craig,
Reid, Charles, Mac, Jeanne, Juan, Roy, Bill,
Jeff, Martin, Jim, Stan and Kim, Reaves,
Ernie, and many others.*

Contents

Acknowledgments

Though a book may have only one author's name on the cover, many people labor to bring it into being. I am deeply indebted to those who have worked, worshiped, and marched beside me; shared their stories; and taken up the tasks of production for this book.

Because this is a book about the local church, I must first thank the members of the Dorchester Temple Baptist Church, where I pastored. They worked with me for peace in our community and in the world. I am particularly grateful for the members of the peacemakers group, who journeyed intimately with me in both the Scriptures and the streets. In other churches in which I have been a member, I have learned various aspects of the peacemaking ministry, sometimes through success and sometimes through failure. I am grateful to all who allowed me to try out various projects with them and to those who challenged me to refine my work.

Many pastors and laypeople from a variety of congregations have shared their stories to enrich this book. Some I approached because I already knew their stories, and others I discovered as I did my research and reviewed the responses to surveys sent out as part of American Baptist Peace Sunday worship packets. I am indebted to all of them for their faithfulness, their creativity, and their willingness to share their stories.

National Ministries, the home mission agency of the American

Baptist Churches, has given me the time and support staff to produce this book. I particularly thank Aidsand Wright-Riggins and Thelma Mitchell for their encouragement and support in undertaking this task. Marjorie Jones has worked with me throughout the production, managing the details, disks, and documents. Andy Smith, Bob Tiller, Ken George, and Diane Giova also helped with feedback, finding stories or checking out my manuscript in their areas of expertise. I am grateful for such colleagues.

The first draft of the book was read by Ken Sehested, Glenda Fontenot, and Dick Myers. Each of them has been a model for me of peacemaking ministry, both in their personal lives and in their local churches. Their comments dramatically improved and enlivened the book, and they cannot be faulted for any of its shortcomings.

The staff at Judson Press have once again been superb to work with. In particular I thank Kristy Pullen, Mary Nicol, Tina Edginton, and Kathleen Hayes, who have labored with me through much of this work.

Introduction

Peacemaking Ministry

"Blessed are the peacemakers," Jesus proclaimed in the Beatitudes, "for they will be called children of God" (Matthew 5:9). Being a peacemaker is a positive activity. Peacemaking is action that is intentionally taken for the purpose of bringing relationships torn by conflict into a condition of genuine reconciliation. Peace doesn't just happen; it is made. People get involved in the complexities and anguish of conflict and must find the threads from which to weave a new bond of justice and harmony.

Peacemakers are called children of God, for by their work they are reflecting the very nature of the One called the God of peace (see Romans 15:33; 16:20; 1 Corinthians 14:33; 2 Corinthians 13:11; Philippians 4:9; 1 Thessalonians 5:23; Hebrews 13:20). God in Christ engaged in the work of reconciliation and then entrusted the Christian community with the "ministry of reconciliation" (2 Corinthians 5:18-20). The reconciliation is forged between God and humanity, between estranged human beings, and between humanity and the entire created order (see Ephesians 2:14-16). When Christians engage in peacemaking and the ministry of reconciliation, we are partners in a central work of God in the world.

The local congregation is a particular manifestation of the body of Christ (see 1 Corinthians 12:27), so it is appropriate for the local congregation to be a locus for peacemaking ministry. As a gathered community of believers, the local church can give flesh to the work of Christ through its witness and action for peace. Peacemaking is not to be surrendered to the realm of politicians, diplomats, and activists; it is to be embraced as a component of the mission of the local church, too.

Conflict affects every dimension of our lives, from interpersonal relationships to international affairs. Wars rage between nations, but they also can rage within our homes. From violence in our streets to violence on our TV screens, we live our conflicts in ways that destroy both our morality and the lives of other human beings. Even when another human's life is not taken, conflict can erode away our personal well-being through fear, rage, bitterness, and stress.

Peacemaking ministry needs to address the full scope of human conflict. We need to minister peace to the wars between nations and the wars between spouses. We need to bring the ministry of reconciliation to conflicted ethnic groups in our communities and conflicted nationalities around the world. We need to speak God's word of peace to the powers that rule the nations and the powers that rule our own hearts. Such peacemaking ministry will touch our inner lives, our close relationships, our lives in our communities, our nation, and our world.

This book can serve as a handbook for peacemaking ministry in the local church. Common elements of congregational life, such as worship, Christian education, and church finances, can become vehicles for peacemaking. The congregation's peace objectives can also be a springboard for mission. Different churches will come to different understandings of God's particular call to them about the ministry of peacemaking. Some churches will act in risky ways that put them at odds with the surrounding culture, while others will risk taking the first steps of getting members to consider Christ's call to peacemaking. No one congregation will be able to do all the peacemaking activities in this book, for that would be both a human impossibility and a dilution of the concentration that is necessary to accomplish anything worthwhile. Whatever the scope and emphasis of your church's peacemaking ministry, this book aims to provide ideas and guidance on how to expand and deepen the spirit and work you and your sisters and brothers undertake for peace in Christ's name.

Reading this book from cover to cover is hardly necessary. Instead of being written as a book you can't put down till you are done, it was written to be a book you will want to pick up again and again. Maybe you will want to look at only one or two chapters at a time, but that is the nature of a handbook. Each chapter focuses on a major aspect of congregational life or a form of peacemaking ministry. In addition to suggesting ideas, the chapters offer stories of the experiences of specific congregations who have developed creative ways to put their convictions into action. There is some overlap of various chapters in order that each can function as a self-contained unit. Some chapters will deal with the dynamics that are unleashed in a congregation and community when people in the church seriously pursue peace efforts. A number of appendices are provided at the end of the book for reference on other resources and organizations involved in peace issues.

Most of the examples are drawn from American Baptist churches, but some stories are included from churches in other countries who have faced their own contexts with special creativity and courage. For those readers who are not Baptists, their own traditions are most likely rich with stories of peacemaking ministry as well. We would all benefit from hearing those stories so we can learn from one another. I trust the stories shared from our American Baptist branch of God's family will help encourage those from other traditions as they seek to be faithful to Christ in light of their own heritage.

Throughout the book I've had local church peacemakers from across the country share their stories and experiences so that more voices than mine can be heard. These first-person accounts are set apart in italics.

Though this book is now in final form, the peacemaking ministry of the local church will never be in final form. New ideas will be generated for peace initiatives. New stories will be lived out that will need telling. New heroes will arise to inspire us in our journey. My hope is that your own church will help write some new chapters in the book of Christians living out the gospel of peace.

Chapter 1

The Sunday Worship Service

The peacemaking ministry of the local church begins and ends in worship. But worship is not confined to a particular room within a building or an hour or two on Sunday. Worship is a whole life lived as an offering to God. The apostle Paul says, "I appeal to you therefore, brothers and sisters, by the mercies of God, to present your bodies as a living sacrifice, holy and acceptable to God, which is your spiritual worship" (Romans 12:1). The entire peacemaking journey for an individual and a congregation can be an act of worship if it is undertaken for Christ. The Sunday service becomes a more explicit and conscious expression of worship that is validated by the larger act of offering one's life in the service of God. What is done in the sanctuary and what is done in the community or across the world are all cut from one cloth of faithful discipleship. So in a fundamental sense this entire book is about worship.

Corporate worship, usually on Sunday for the local church, is the shared experience of the members of the congregation before God. We gather together in the name and in the presence of Jesus Christ, and in that gathering we give expression to our faith, our values, our community, and our discipleship. The energizing source of our peacemaking can come through worship, sending us into the world with divine purpose and power to be agents of reconciliation, justice, and healing. Then we come back from our particular labors to reflect back to God all our experiences in the journey. When the fullness of peace comes in God's time, worship will continue.

We come to the Sunday worship service as we are, bringing all the confusion and pains of our conflicts with us. In worship we can lift up what is tearing at us or what is destroying people about whom we care. We can question; we can cry; we can intercede through prayer. We also come seeking a "word from God" to address our needs and our situation. We can listen in the silence of prayer, in the message of the preacher, and in the words we sing. We can gain nourishment from new aspects of God's call to peacemaking for our minds to ponder throughout the week. We can gain nourishment for our inner being to go back and face whatever challenges are presenting themselves to us.

We can celebrate the goodness of God with praise, reveling joyfully in the redemptive works of God in our lives and in the lives of others. Most of all, worship can be an opportunity to connect with the heart of God. God is referred to in the Bible as the "God of peace" (1 Thessalonians 5:23). In fact, in Judges 6:24 Gideon builds an altar called "Yahweh *is* peace" (italics mine), a characterization of God parallel to John's "God is love" (1 John 4:16). Peace is announced at the birth of Jesus, then bestowed by the risen Christ upon his followers (Luke 2:14; John 14:27; 20:19). Peace is the culmination of God's work in history (Isaiah 2:2-4). *Shalom*, the Hebrew word for peace, expresses the fullness of God's redemptive purpose in human history.[1] In worship we bind ourselves to the heart of the divine One who is peace and who works peace. We prepare ourselves to be more active participants in God's redemptive project in human history. We are shaped deep within so that our peacemaking is not a mere cause or ideology but is an expression of passion for the One who made and redeemed us. Worship grounds our peacemaking in the infinite depths of the heart of God.

Because of who God is and what we are called to be and do as Christians, peace concerns should naturally be a part of the wor-

---

[1]See Isaiah 55:10-13; 65:17-25. Also see Paul D. Hanson's "War and Peace in the Hebrew Bible," *Interpretation, A Journal of Bible and Theology*, October 1984, 341. The "American Baptist Policy Statement on Peace" (available from National Ministries Literature Resources, P.O. Box 851, Valley Forge, PA 19482) discusses the biblical/theological basis for peace.

shiping experience of a local church. Often "peace" is left unmentioned because of a fear of controversy, except for inner peace or interpersonal peace. But to limit our worship by excluding peace at the places of profound conflict and anguish, including global conflict, is to deny God's sovereignty over all dimensions of our lives and histories. Bringing our conflicts and God's call to peacemaking into our worship experience both rounds out our Christian faith and provides a spiritual resource for people in the congregation to address points of crisis and need.

Prayer As Peace Work

Corporate prayer is a regular part of our worship services and can be an opportunity for voicing our concerns for peace. The pastor or worship leader can take the leading role, but other members can lead in prayer for peace concerns if there are opportunities to voice requests or to offer prayers in the service.

We are instructed in the Bible to pray for government leaders so that we may live quiet and peaceable lives (1 Timothy 2:2). That means praying for policies conducive to peace with other nations and with the citizenry. It means praying for the success of negotiations to resolve conflicts without violence. When President Reagan and Soviet President Gorbachev were preparing for their summit in 1985, the members of Prescott Memorial Baptist Church in Memphis, Tennessee, sent a telegram to each leader encouraging him in the quest to halt the arms race and offering their prayers on behalf of the negotiations. During the days before the Gulf War, hundreds of churches had special services of prayer for peace, often including fasting. At points of decision making for our own nation or for other nations, such as in the Middle East or former Yugoslavia or Korea, we can include in the corporate prayer intercession for God to give national leaders the wisdom and courage to act for peace.

Intercession is frequently made for family members in the armed forces, which is appropriate since they are our loved ones. In times of crisis or war, they are at a special risk, both physically and in terms of their total personhood. In war many people take actions or undergo experiences that can affect them for life, and we can plead for God to shape those moments toward wholeness not destruction. We also are explicitly told by Jesus to pray for our enemies

(Matthew 5:44). This kind of prayer separates true followers of Jesus from practitioners of civil religion. During the Gulf War many congregations remembered the suffering of the soldiers and citizens of Iraq as well as their own family members and friends involved in the war. As Mark Twain pointed out with his caustic wit in "The War Prayer," "If you would beseech a blessing upon yourself, beware! lest without intent you invoke a curse upon a neighbor at the same time."[2] To pray for success for our side means death and destruction for those on the other side—children orphaned, bodies maimed, spouses widowed, sorrows multiplied. Jesus calls his followers to transcend the narrow focus on our own side in a conflict and to see the humanity and the need of those who are our adversaries.

Praying for the enemy can also address people closer to home: people in different ethnic groups when a community is in conflict; people on different sides of labor disputes during a strike; gang members terrorizing our neighborhoods; abusive bosses or family members; even members of our congregation with whom we fervently disagree. We have enemies whose faces are known to us. In the times of corporate prayer, a pastor can lead the people in learning how to pray for enemies. Pray to be given God's eyes. What need does God see? What hurt does God see? What fear in that other person's heart is known to God? What is the good that God intends to come into that person's life? Those are matters for prayer, perhaps voiced generically by the worship leader but given specific content by each person in the pew. In the end, we may find that God's greatest work is to change our own hearts. Christian peacemaker Jim Wallis says that "fervent prayer for our enemies is a great obstacle to war and the feelings that lead to it."[3] What I bring knowingly or unknowingly to fuel a conflict can be surprisingly touched by God when I pray for my enemies.

Often in our times of prayer we remember our missionaries and others engaged in sharing God's love through word and deed. We

---

[2]Mark Twain [pen name of Samuel Clemens], "The War Prayer," *Peace-Work*, no. 1, 1991, 1.

[3]Jim Wallis, ed., "The Work of Prayer," *Waging Peace: A Handbook for the Struggle to Abolish Nuclear Weapons* (New York: Harper & Row, 1982), 196.

can pray for the peacemakers as God's agents of reconciliation, even as we pray for missionaries. In fact, many of our missionaries are engaged in peacemaking and reconciliation ministries themselves.[4] Peacemaking is a mission with a divine blessing. Peacemakers are often in vulnerable places, for they enter a conflict between the adversarial parties, where emotions can run high and, in some cases, where violence is frequent. Pray for church leaders in countries with civil wars. Pray for church leaders in communities with civil unrest, such as gang violence, riots, strikes or lockouts, and ethnic conflict. Prayers can be offered on their behalf for wisdom, creativity, protection, and courage.

We may not know about particular peacemakers in a conflict. Little news has come out of the work of peacemakers in former Yugoslavia. In Bosnia, a Croatian Catholic priest and some monks interposed themselves between the Croat militia and Muslim villagers fearful of being victims of "ethnic cleansing."[5] These courageous peacemakers were able to quench the fires of violence in their immediate community. Such brothers and sisters may be unknown to us, but we can still pray for them. When we pray about a conflict in the news that disturbs us, we can pray specifically for God's people in the midst of that setting, that they may be given all the grace they need to be agents of reconciliation and peace.

As someone who has engaged in a peacemaking venture in another country,[6] I have personally known the power of prayer by people interceding on my behalf. God has opened doors where there seemed not even to be a doorway. Praying for peace and for peacemakers is a peacemaking ministry in and of itself. Our prayer is peace work, for in the divine mystery of prayer it undergirds peacemakers with God's power and wisdom, as well as giving God an opportunity to do a work for peace within our own hearts.

One way to make a peace prayer is through the planting of a "peace pole." The peace pole has the international peace prayer

---

[4]See, for example, the story of Gustavo Parajón in my book *Christian Peacemaking: From Heritage to Hope* (Valley Forge, Pa.: Judson Press, 1994), 132-135.

[5]Reported in the video "Hope for Bosnia: Beyond the News," produced by the Mennonite Central Committee.

[6]See *Christian Peacemaking: From Heritage to Hope, 139-143.*

written in various languages: "May peace prevail on earth."[7] A church can plant a pole outside or set it up on a stand in the sanctuary, foyer, or fellowship hall. The First Baptist Church of Detroit concluded their Vacation Bible School one year by planting a peace pole. Many local churches around the world can be found with a peace pole in their building or on their property.

Music

Many hymns in our heritage use stridently militaristic images, such as "Onward, Christian Soldiers" and "Stand Up, Stand Up for Jesus, Ye Soldiers of the Cross." Though these hymns reflect military imagery found in the Bible, when religion is used in service of a nation's war ventures, the line between spiritual imagery and propaganda can easily evaporate. There are, however, many hymns that have a rich peacemaking message. Appendix A lists hymns that have peace themes and are found in most major hymnals. Use of these hymns, even in services with themes other than peace, such as world missions, can help give voice to constructive images for our discipleship.

The first Christmas carol was a peace hymn; the angelic host sang to the shepherds about Jesus' birth, "On earth peace among those whom he favors!" (Luke 2:14). "It Came Upon the Midnight Clear," the last verse of "O Come, O Come, Emmanuel," and "While Shepherds Watched Their Flocks by Night" all give voice to peace themes as part of the Christmas message. "I Heard the Bells on Christmas Day" presents a debate between hope and despair that resonates with the struggle for integrity amid the ongoing violence of our world. "O Holy Night" has a third verse with a message of liberation worthy of being underlined. When an Advent or Christmas service is built around a peace theme, such carols will enhance the message.

Congregation members can be encouraged to write their own hymns related to peace. Some with musical talent may be able to compose original music for the lyrics. Such a hymn could be taught to the choir and then introduced through the choir to the congrega-

---

[7]For more information or to order a peace pole, contact Peace Pole Makers, U.S.A., 3534 Lanham Rd., Maple City, MI 49664 (616-334-4567; fax 616-334-4523).

tion as a whole. If someone is a good wordsmith but not a composer, a familiar hymn tune can be selected to go with new words. If the congregation responds well to the hymn, it should be copyrighted as well as sent to the denominational peace office to be used as a resource for other congregations.

There are many excellent contemporary musical compositions focused on peace themes, from hymns to choral numbers. Jane Parker Huber's *A Singing Faith*[8] is one of the best collections available for combining contemporary lyrics on peace-and-justice themes with familiar hymn tunes. A host of hymns and Scripture songs can be found in the multiplicity of songbooks available in any Christian bookstore. Some of these have filtered into the newer hymnals, but sadly not as many of the new hymns related to Christian social concerns, including peace, have been given attention in the musical mainstream. It takes a bit more detective work to build up a collection of contemporary songs related to peace, but they are available.

Any copyrighted material used for congregational singing should be handled appropriately. Even using a hymn in a bulletin insert or on an overhead transparency should be done only with permission. Copyright services are available to facilitate this process; the church pays an annual fee and reports the hymns used in the service's listing.[9] This will probably cover the bulk of hymns you want to use, but not all of them. For those that are not covered by the copyright service, you will have to track down the publishing house or the author—whichever holds the copyright. If the hymn has been published, the publishing house will have the author's address if he or she holds the copyright. Such effort may not be worth it if a hymn is to be used only once.

Your church may want to consider production of a supplemental hymnal if you don't have one already. A supplement can enable a church to publish and use hymns that pick up social concerns themes, including peace, which are often given short shrift in hymnals. The supplement could also contain favorite hymns not

---

[8]Jane Parker Huber, *A Singing Faith* (Philadelphia: Westminster, 1987).

[9]A major copyright service is Christian Copyright Licensing, Inc. (CCLI), 6130 NE 78th Ct., Suite C-11, Portland, OR 97218-2853 (800-234-2446; fax 502-257-2244).

found in the church's hymnal, standard hymns redone with inclusive language, and compositions from members of the congregation. When printing your own supplemental songbook, you should of course obtain permission for the inclusion of each hymn either from the author or from the publishing house, depending on who holds the copyright. Central Baptist Church in Wayne, Pennsylvania, developed its own "Uncommon Book of Worship." It contains hymns from a variety of sources, for which the church diligently obtained the appropriate permissions. Some of the hymns are by congregational members. They also included readings for worship use. The "Uncommon Book of Worship" is in loose-leaf form so that every few years it can be updated.

Liturgy and Ceremony

For many people ritualized expressions of our faith, such as the corporate acts of liturgy and symbolic ceremonies, add a special richness to worship. Litanies are frequently produced in denominational worship resources along with other liturgical aids.[10] Litanies can also be written to give particular expression to the contemporary concerns of the world and the congregation. It is important, however, not to preach at people through the litanies; rather, try to express the heart of people who are reaching out to God from the realities in which the church members live. Words that are not true to those who voice them do not advance the worship experience but only raise questions of hypocrisy. Peacemaking in worship must be honest, in line with the prophetic exhortation to "love *truth* and peace" (Zechariah 8:19, italics mine). Confessions that name our own sins can bring healing, so carefully examine every confession used to see that it expresses with integrity where people in the congregation are in their spiritual journey.

The Lord's Supper, or Communion, is a liturgical ceremony that is fundamental both to our faith expression and to the meaning of peace for Christians. Ephesians 2:13-16 says:

---

[10] See the worship resources produced annually for Peace Sunday by the American Baptist Peace Program. The Presbyterian Peacemaking Program has also produced a two-volume resource, *Peacemaking Through Worship,* which contains litanies, prayers, readings, and other worship aids. Addresses are in Appendix B.

But now in Christ Jesus you who once were far off have been brought near by the blood of Christ. For he is our peace; in his flesh he has made both groups into one and has broken down the dividing wall, that is, the hostility between us. He has abolished the law with its commandments and ordinances, that he might create in himself one new humanity in place of the two, thus making peace, and might reconcile both groups to God in one body through the cross, thus putting to death that hostility through it.

Christ's sacrifice becomes the bond of peace between Christians, so every time we gather around the Lord's table we are celebrating that peace. Such unity can be affirmed explicitly as a peace witness through the words that introduce the time of Communion or in the prayers for the bread and cup. World Communion Sunday (the first Sunday in October) gives an excellent occasion to remember the global bonds of peace forged at the cross, no matter what the political alignments of our national governments.[11] World Communion Sunday is a colorful and festive occasion at the First Baptist Church of Greater Cleveland.

We use the opportunity of World Communion Sunday to get at the heart of the relationship between peace and global consciousness. On that occasion, we fill the nave with flags of the nations, sing songs that call us to barrier breaking, utilize various languages in a litany sometimes led by persons dressed in the clothing of their native lands, and intentionally provide a mixture of various colors, textures, and national origins of breads for our Communion service.
                        —Gilbert Hellwig, Cleveland, Ohio

Many congregations conclude their observance of the Lord's Supper by singing "Blest Be the Tie That Binds." If the congregation has some racial or ethnic diversity, the breaking down of those social dividing walls can be visually enhanced if the participants form a circle around the sanctuary. Forming a circle breaks the worshiper out of the solitary experience of Communion and allows each person to scan the wondrous diversity of people called into this particular portion of God's family.

Some congregations have given a tangible expression to that

---

[11]For Baptists, another occasion for expressing explicit global unity through the cross is Baptist World Alliance Sunday, the first Sunday in February.

diversity by exchanging Communion glasses with congregations in other countries when members travel on friendship or mission tours. When a U.S. church celebrated the Lord's Supper with a glass from a Moscow congregation during the Cold War, the congregation made a powerful witness to the transcending reconciling power of their one Lord. In the era of plastic disposable cups, this symbolism can be retained through placing a gift chalice or cup on the Communion table.

The ringing of bells has also been used in conjunction with various peace observances. Bells have been tolled in remembrance of the Holocaust. Churches with bells can ring them in celebration of peace events or in calling people to special times of prayer.

At Park Street Baptist Church in Pittsfield, New Hampshire, Peace Sunday was celebrated by inviting each worshiper to ring the church bell as a symbol of his or her commitment to personal peace.

In the morning message I stressed the biblical model for individuals to follow in order to be at peace with other individuals. According to Matthew 5:23-26, if we know we've wronged someone else, it is up to us to go and make things right. And Matthew 18:15-20 tells us that if someone has wronged us, it's still our responsibility to go and be reconciled to them—not to stew in anger.

The congregation's witness for peace was advertised in the newspaper during the previous two weeks so the community would understand the significance of the bell ringing.

—Jeff Collins, Pittsfield, New Hampshire

Lights also have been used symbolically as a sign of hope amid dark times. Lights have been used in many worship services, vigils, and demonstrations, including in the East German churches. Prodemocracy demonstrations began in the East German churches with prayer services followed by candlelight marches into the town centers. In the United States, prayer vigils during the days before the Gulf War were often held by candlelight. One congregation reflected Japanese tradition during an anniversary of the Hiroshima bombing by sending lit floating candles down the neighboring river.

When all the rich avenues of expression in worship are used to express God's call to peace, then our spirituality and the conflicted world in which we live are integrated. God's grace is given an opportunity to permeate our lives at points of pain, confusion, and anger. Hope can be energized to lead us from the Sunday service of worship to the various spheres of our lives where God's peace is needed.

Chapter 2

Preaching on Peace

The ministry of preaching is a central part of the worship experience of a congregation. Preaching involves the interpretation of God's Word in the contemporary context, bridging the gap of centuries between Bible days and today. As such, effective preaching needs to stand on two legs: one planted on the Bible and the historical revelation of God through Jesus Christ, Israel, and the early church; the other planted on the realities of life for the members of the local congregation. Each week the preacher has the opportunity to make the ancient Word a contemporary, living Word.

Preaching Peacefully

That Word has been described in the Bible as the "gospel of peace" (Ephesians 6:15). Peace was woven into the message of Jesus, from the angelic proclamation at his birth to the commissioning he gave his disciples following the Resurrection. Preaching on peace themes flows out of the core understanding of the message to be delivered.

Many pastors, however, find it difficult to preach on peace because it can be controversial whenever one ventures beyond the sphere of inner peace or peace in our interpersonal relationships. Addressing areas of conflict in the community, nation, or world inevitably plunges one into controversy, as people and groups line up on different sides with competing interests that are near and dear to them. If those sides are represented in the congregation, the preacher is entering a mine field to speak from the pulpit in any way that touches on the concerns in the conflict.

Controversy is no excuse for silence, however. The preacher is one called by God to speak God's message to the people. Faithfulness to that calling is essential if the preacher is to be worth his or her salt. That does not mean one must be a shrill, self-righteous prophet, abusing the congregants and the pulpit for political agendas. The preacher in the local congregation is a pastor, so the word needs to come out of a heart and mind that is deeply committed to nurturing people in their faith journeys. The message of peace needs to be spoken in the context of love and mutual respect between pastor and people; otherwise the preacher is not practicing what is preached!

So how does one preach on peace without falling into the traps of superficiality on the one hand or stridency on the other? Kyle Childress, pastor of the Austin Heights Baptist Church in Nacogdoches, Texas, has some good advice in his article "How to Preach on Peace (Without Resorting to Violence)."[1] Childress calls us to preach biblically. Biblically based preaching gives the congregants the spiritual and ethical perspective from which to approach the issues that they face. In all the confusion and complexity of the modern world, people want to hear a word from God that can provide clear guidance. Differences might exist over the application of the biblical values to a particular issue, but effective dialogue and spiritual growth can take place when people are challenged to deal with what the Bible says. Preaching on peace should be not less biblical because it deals with peace concerns but *more* biblical because such a message goes against much of the world-view ingrained in our society.

The preacher must also preach prayerfully. In controversial issues it is tempting to speak one's own word rather than God's. So the sermon must be constructed out of prayer. God's peace must come into the preacher's heart before it can flow to the congregation in restorative power. Does the preacher have an ax to grind with a

---

[1]*PeaceWork*, March/April 1986, 6-7. *PeaceWork* is a newsletter published by the Baptist Peace Fellowship for North America.

contrary-minded church member? "Take it to the Lord in prayer."
Prayer will also help the preacher connect with God's heart, which
is deeply grieved by the sorrows that human conflict and war bring.
Out of such prayer a message with depth and grace can emerge.
Besides preaching from the Bible, the preacher can draw people
into the message through stories. Stories allow people to identify
with other people as they face situations and decisions. Rather than
moralizing—"do this" and "don't do this"—the preacher, through
the use of story, invites the listener to wrestle with the dilemmas of
being faithful in situations that may not be clear cut. Such stories
can be gathered from missionary newsletters, magazines such as *The
Baptist Peacemaker* and *Sojourners*, and direct experiences through
one's travels, conferences, or involvements in the community.

Childress speaks of the timing of preaching on peace. Sermons
should emerge out of the pastoral relationship. Instead of shocking
people on Sunday morning with a politically loaded sermon, talk
with people in their kitchens and living rooms and wrestle with them
through the issues in Sunday school classes and Bible studies.

*I learned very early that there were two keys to my being able
to preach on controversial subjects like peacemaking. First, my
sermons were strongly biblical, usually narratives, and they were
rarely "topical." In other words, peacemaking arose out of the
normal preaching of the biblical material over time rather than
being a specific subject in search of a text. Second and perhaps
most important, I spent a great deal of time personally visiting with
the members of the congregation, talking, struggling, and wres-
tling with them about peacemaking, pointing out that the way
they dealt with conflict with their son-in-law and what we did
about the arms race were both connected to being disciples of
Jesus. My pastoral visits were rarely boring.*
—*Kyle Childress, Nacogdoches, Texas*

Take time and be patient with people. As Childress says, "People
need to know we are not there trying to convince them of something,
but we are there because we care for them. We love them for who
they are and not for who we can make them into."[2]

When the preaching is done against something—such as a governmental policy—the likelihood of resistance is increased. If

[2] Ibid., 7.

someone is in agreement with that policy, then the sermon comes across as an attack, and the normal response to being attacked is to get defensive. The preacher has then set up an adversarial relationship with the person in the pew. A positive approach is more likely to encourage open-minded consideration of new ideas and approaches to a problem. Take a problem-solving tack, presenting a constructive vision for peace, reconciliation, or justice. There may be a critique in the positive vision, but this kind of an approach invites the hearer to enter into the challenge of resolving the issue and finding a way out of the dilemma. The hearer is then more likely to feel stretched in faith, which can be a positive experience, rather than attacked for disagreeing with the pastor.

Sometimes peace topics can be very sobering and sorrowful for a congregation to face, such as Holocaust Sunday, the anniversaries of the atomic bombings, or when a slaughter such as took place in Rwanda fills the news. To honestly face these kinds of events, especially when we are complicit in them, can be very disturbing to congregants who come with expectations of being lifted up and encouraged by the message. Facing human evil, in the world and in ourselves, is never an easy matter, but to ignore it will leave us with an insipid, shallow faith. To help church members both grapple with the realities of evil and move constructively with the preacher, it is important to convey God's grace and hope as well as to direct congregants into appropriate opportunities for response. If people are made to look at evil and feel guilty about it too often, they will feel the preacher is "beating up on them." Such preaching is ultimately disempowering for people. Grace and hope must be strong elements of the message if the hearers are to gain the strength and commitment to become "doers of the word," especially in the face of grave evil.

Biblical Texts for Preaching Peace

A number of biblical texts may immediately come to mind when one thinks of preaching on peace.[3] "Blessed are the peacemakers"

---

[3]"God Intends Shalom: Scriptures Which Speak of God's Promised Future" is a collection of Bible passages from Genesis to Revelation on peace themes. It is available from the Baptist Peace Fellowship of North America. See address in Appendix B.

(Matthew 5:9) gives an explicit statement of God's valuing of this work. Jesus weeping over Jerusalem in Luke 19:41-44 because they did not recognize "the things that make for peace" provides a vivid picture of the heart of God in relation to the warring and violence on our planet. The prophetic vision of swords being beaten into plowshares and nations learning war no more (Isaiah 2:2-4 and Micah 4:1-5) presents God's future—a future that certainly stands in vivid contrast to the present. Such texts make clear sermon themes and need to be preached. Unfortunately, many of these texts are so familiar to some in our churches that they are trivialized and not taken seriously in the real-world conflicts with which people grapple. The challenge is to present them in such a way that people will take seriously the call to flesh out these biblical concerns.

A number of passages speak to the deeper issues in peacemaking. Hosea 10:13-15 and Psalm 33:16-17 deal with the issue of trust. In what do we find our security? Hosea 14:1-3 makes a clear contrast between trusting in military alliances and trusting in God. The tie can be made from these prophetic passages to Jesus' statement in the Garden of Gethsemane that "all who take the sword will perish by the sword" (Matthew 26:52). Jesus' challenge to "love your enemies" (Matthew 5:43) pushes the disciple into a deep examination of his or her own heart and how we create enemies and nourish enmity.

The ministry of reconciliation to which Paul calls Christians in 2 Corinthians 5:18-19 is based on Christ's own reconciling work. The peacemaking of Jesus can be a theme for a Communion meditation by drawing on Ephesians 2:14-16, where Christ is presented as "our peace," who "in his flesh . . . has made both groups into one and has broken down the dividing wall, that is, the hostility between us."

Specific biblical case studies in conflict resolution can illustrate the skills needed to peacefully bring our conflicts to a constructive conclusion. Many biblical conflicts are horribly and often bloodily resolved, sowing seeds for further enmity and violence. But there are some examples of good processes that can instruct Christians on conflict resolution skills for their own lives. The early church resolved its first conflict in Acts 6 by addressing a situation of injustice with structural change and the empowerment of those who had been disenfranchised. Joshua 22:10-34 presents an obscure but fascinating story of conflict resolution in which the two sides averted a war by carefully communicating through their false projections of the other side's motives. The story is too long and culturally alien to be done in a straight expository format, but creative storytelling could bring to life a lesson usually ignored.

A very different approach to take in preaching is to use a familiar story symbolically. Abraham offering Isaac on the altar is a graphic and gripping story that can raise the question of how we offer our children on the altar. In a society where children are killing each other with guns to the extent that homicide is the leading cause of childhood death, are we not sacrificing the next generation? For what reason? Will we hear the voice calling us to stop before it is too late?

Familiarizing oneself with the extensive biblical material on war and peace will open up many new avenues to approach peacemaking themes from the pulpit.[4] Sometimes what we draw out of the Bible depends on the questions we bring to it. If we come with questions about living faithfully and constructively in a world of injustice and violence, familiar passages will shine with new meaning and forgotten passages will spring out with surprising potency.

Using Illustrations

Peace can be promoted in sermons that don't speak directly to peace by using illustrations. A sermon on prayer can use illustrations of the power of prayer in Jimmy Carter's Camp David peace process or in negotiations among gang members at the "gang summit" in 1993[5] or in stories from your own experiences in peacemaking. A sermon on hope can be illustrated by the power of hope in those who struggled nonviolently for justice, peace, and freedom, from Martin Luther King, Jr., and the civil rights movement in the United States to Nelson Mandela and the freedom movement in South

---

[4] My *Bible Study Guide on War and Peace* (Valley Forge, Pa.: National Ministries, 1990) is a comprehensive workbook on biblical passages dealing with war and peace (available in English or Spanish). See resources listing at the end of the book.

[5] These stories and others involving prayer and peacemaking are told in my book *Christian Peacemaking: From Heritage to Hope* (Valley Forge, Pa.: Judson Press, 1994).

Africa. Reading the stories of peacemaking in books such as my *Christian Peacemaking* or Paul Dekar's *For the Healing of the Nations* or the contemporary stories gleaned from the news will provide a wealth of examples of love, courage, faith, communication, perseverance, and even miracle.

Small details from personal experiences involved in peacemaking can make compelling stories to illustrate matters besides peace and justice. When my family and I were going to a demonstration about the war in Central America our four-year-old son, Chris, asked my wife and me if we had prayed about the war. I responded in a condescending way, "Of course we have prayed about the war." Chris asked if we could pray right then for peace, so we stopped on the sidewalk, and he poured out his little heart to God: "God, help President Reagan to stop making the war in Nicaragua." I was so busy acting that I didn't take prayer seriously, but Chris, in the childlike purity of his faith, did. His prayer is a marvelous example of the faith of a child that Jesus said is necessary to have to enter the kingdom of heaven (Matthew 18:3). In a sermon on church renewal that deals with becoming like children, Chris' peace prayer is a clear illustration of faith. Peacemaking here is just a normal activity of life in which one can see many other aspects of the Christian journey portrayed. Treating it as something to be experienced in the normal flow of our lives helps congregants move peace-and-justice work from the fringe of Christian action to the center of living out one's faith.

Opportunities in the Church Year

The church year provides many opportunities to speak on peace, both the traditional Christian seasons and the special days from our national or denominational experience. Lent and Holy Week provide many opportunities to examine the sins in ourselves that lead to hatred and violence as well as to affirm the reconciling work of Christ on the cross. James 4 speaks of the sins that lead to war, so a Lenten journey of repentance can give focused attention to the expression of those sins in our own lives and culture. Jesus weeping over Jerusalem is a major part of the Palm Sunday event. Pentecost was the time when God's Spirit overcame the divisiveness of Babel and gave a peacemaking message to a society torn with racial and ethnic conflicts. Advent and Christmas present us with the coming of the "Prince of Peace," at whose birth the angels proclaimed "on earth peace" (Luke 2:14). The Magnificat of Mary (Luke 1:46-55) and Herod's slaughter of the innocents (Matthew 2:16-18) speak with power when viewed through the contemporary experience of poor countries in Africa, Latin America, and Asia.

The Fourth of July presents a challenge on how a Christian relates to the nation. Jesus said his kingdom was not of this world (John 18:36), but many congregations may be tempted to make the Fourth of July a festival of civil religion. This can be a good time to look at God's claims over the nations and those who hold positions of leadership. National elections can also be a time to examine such values through biblical lenses. Memorial Day presents similar concerns, with the added burden that many people in our congregations have served in the military or lost friends and loved ones in wars. Nancy Sehested, pastor of Prescott Memorial Baptist Church in Memphis, Tennessee, preached about the lessons learned from soldiers—their dedication, their discipline, their willingness to die for others—while raising the question of what the dead would say if they could speak to us now. Would they wonder if they died so humanity could wage bigger and more destructive wars? Would they wonder why their sacrifice has not caused us to learn other ways to settle our disputes?[6]

Mother's Day was first called for by Julia Ward Howe in 1872 as an explicit protest against war. After witnessing the horrors of the Civil War in the United States and the Franco-Prussian War in Europe, Julia Ward Howe called women to arise: "Our husbands shall not come to us, reeking with carnage, for caresses and applause. Our sons shall not be taken from us to unlearn all that we have been able to teach them of charity, mercy and patience. We women of one country will be too tender to those of another country to allow our sons to be trained to injure theirs."[7] Such a call is a far cry from the sentimentality that marks most of our Mother's Day observances.

Martin Luther King, Jr., Day in January honors a church hero

---

[6]Nancy Hastings Sehested, "Let the Silence of Cemeteries End," *The Baptist Peacemaker*, Spring 1990, 18.

[7]"Mother's Day, 1870," *PeaceWork*, January-April 1988, 1.

who made a national, and even global, impact with his ministry of nonviolent action for justice and peace. Preaching on the life and work of King, along with the biblical teaching that shaped him, can weave a thread from the days of Jesus through the civil rights movement to contemporary concerns in shaping a more just society. Issues of racial justice, reconciliation, and community peace will continue to require the raising of prophetic and pastoral voices throughout our lifetimes.

Holocaust Remembrance Day provides another occasion to speak on prejudice and racial violence. The date to commemorate the slaughter of six million Jews and other victims of Nazi hatred is set by the chief rabbinate of Israel each year. Christian remembrance is important due to Christian complicity in anti-Semitism, including Nazi Germany and the United States. In humility and with repentant hearts church members can commit themselves to the pledge "Never again!" The anniversaries of the dropping of the atomic bombs on August 6 and 9 remind us of the human potential for self-extinction and the abyss at whose edge we have flirted. The memorial to Sadako, the girl from Hiroshima who died from radiation-induced leukemia, is inscribed: "This is our cry, this is our prayer: Peace in the world."

American Baptists observe Peace Sunday on the first Sunday in May, and usually a resource packet is produced by the national staff to assist in congregational programming and worship preparation. Many other denominations have similar dates set aside in their calendars (such as the Presbyterians' Peacemaking Offering). World Communion Sunday, observed on the first Sunday of October, provides an occasion to focus on our ties with all people in God's family across any of the boundaries of human enmity. The Lord's table is the place where Christ's peace between us is symbolically actualized. The interfaith observance of Peace with Justice Week is held at the end of October.

In planning a year's preaching, a pastor can select some of these occasions to expand the congregation's understanding of God's concern for peace and justice and to raise the ethical challenges of responding to God's concerns in today's contexts.[8] Various aspects

---

[8] The Baptist Peace Fellowship of North America periodically publishes an extensive calendar of dates, anniversaries, and events that are of significance for peace preaching and programming. See address in Appendix B.

of peacemaking can be addressed so that the message doesn't become redundant and grating. Tying peace issues to major symbols and celebrations of our faith also deepens their meaning with integrity. We haven't fully presented the meaning of Communion unless at some point we speak of the reconciliation that Christ's sacrifice requires us to make with each other. We haven't explored repentance during Lent unless we face the sins that breed war and violence. Martin Luther said, "If you preach the Gospel in all aspects with the exception of the issues which deal specifically with your time, you are not preaching the Gospel at all."[9] Sound preaching, then, will address contemporary concerns of peace and justice, and these dates throughout the church year provide many excellent opportunities to heed Luther's words.

---

[9] Quoted in *Post-American*, Summer 1972, 1.

Chapter 3

Christian Education: Children and Youth

Ken Sehested of the Baptist Peace Fellowship of North America compares our peacemaking to growing pumpkins. Pumpkins are seasonal; you plant the seed, care for the vine as it grows, then harvest the pumpkins in due time. Working on major peace issues is like growing pumpkins: you work on them for a time, then move on to the next concern.

On the other hand, Ken likens raising children to growing date trees. A farmer plants a date tree by faith and a hope that is far-seeing. A date tree takes many years to reach its fruit-bearing stage. The farmer may even have died by the time the first harvest of dates is ready. But the date farmer has a long-range vision and a commitment to growth even if it takes time. What we teach our children may not bear fruit for a long time. But the biblical promise is like that of the farmer growing dates: "Train children in the right way, and when old, they will not stray" (Proverbs 22:6). Parents often wait a long time to see the fruit in their children, but in faith and hope they provide nurture and care so that their young ones will get off to a healthy start in life.

Peacemaking ministry among our children, therefore, is a long-term but vitally important part of any church's work toward the day when the lion shall lie down with the lamb. It is also a ministry that is vital to counter the trends toward violence in American society. Children today are growing up in one of the most violent cultures ever. Over five thousand children a year die from handgun violence, and the Harvard School of Public Health reported that the rate of children wounded by gunshots doubled from 1987 to 1990. Psychologists have found that children growing up in Chicago's public-housing projects were showing the same psychological stress symptoms as children growing up in the war zones of Mozambique, Cambodia, and Nicaragua.[1] A survey of one thousand Chicago high school and elementary students showed that nearly 40 percent had witnessed a shooting, 33 percent a stabbing, and 25 percent a murder.[2] For those not in the most violent neighborhoods, a steady diet of violence is still available from television, movies, and video games. Violence is an easily accessible thrill for children.[3]

Christian education is faced with the task of overcoming this violent worldliness with a gospel-oriented counterculture that helps youth enter into the adult world as people who can make a positive difference. "Growing date trees" for peace and justice is done in a very harsh environment—but we can be encouraged by the fact that God is the One who gives the growth. No doubt our children and youth will continue to astonish us with their insights and dedication to follow God's call and do what is right. Clearly the staggering needs of children in our society indicate that we have much work to do—and need more workers—if the next generation is to have a hopeful future and the skills to build it.

Peace Parenting

Nobody has more impact on growing the date trees of a young person's life than his or her parents. Therefore, Christian education takes place first and foremost in the home. Parents can be teachers

---

[1] See James Garbarino, Kathleen Kostelny, and Nancy Dubrow, *No Place to Be a Child: Growing Up in a War Zone* (Lexington, Mass.: Lexington Books, 1991).

[2] Ibid., 136.

[3] The Children's Defense Fund (25 E St., NW, Washington, DC 20001 [202-662-3589]) is a leading advocacy group for children, particularly on issues related to violence. The annual Children's Sabbath materials produced by CDF can be incorporated into the Christian education program, worship services, and advocacy actions of the church.

of peace through all the forms of communication and shared living whereby our values are passed from one generation to the next. Children learn more from parents' behavior than words, so parents need to model peacemaking in their lifestyles, in how they handle relational conflicts, in how they treat their children, and in how they live as global citizens. Peacemaking behavior by parents provides their children a tangible reference point for the spoken words and handed-down stories that interpret the values being lived out.

Parenting in a way that raises a child to contribute to peace and justice in the world is a difficult challenge. Parenting for peace and justice is a topic of sufficient scope that numerous books have been written on it—and even an organization formed to support and educate parents. Parenting for Peace and Justice (PPJ) is a network that grew out of the Institute for Peace and Justice in St. Louis, Missouri. Jim and Kathy McGinnis developed a training program that has resulted in thousands of families over the last decade learning parenting skills that will build values that foster peace and justice, from the most intimate relationships to one's involvement in the global community. PPJ holds training events around the country for clusters of churches in a metro area.[4] A congregation can send a couple or family to the training session, who can return with both the skills and resources to conduct similar training in their own congregation. This multiplies the impact of the education, touching more families than one organization could ever reach directly. PPJ also has video and print resources for use in a church training program if no one can attend a regional training event. A church library can also make some of these and other outstanding parenting and family conflict resolution resources available for parents' use.

Teaching and practicing conflict resolution skills within the family provides peacemaking skills that can be carried over into all arenas of life. Beginning with children at home ensures that these skills will be woven into the value system the family nurtures and that they will have plenty of practice in putting them to use. The McGinnises encourage family meetings on a regular basis. Regular

---

[4]For information about Parenting for Peace and Justice training events or to obtain resources, contact PPJ at 4144 Lindell Blvd., St. Louis, MO 63108 (314-533-4445). They also produce an excellent newsletter for parents.

meetings to deal with family issues, with a posted agenda that anyone can add to, give family members a constructive setting in which to work out their conflicts. Basic communication and negotiation skills—giving everyone a chance to speak, restating what others have said, making sure decisions are clear, and looking for "win/win" solutions—can be taught in church training programs and then put into practice at home.

Family worship and the church calendar can be used to teach about peace-and-justice heros. All Saints Day (November 1) provides an excellent opportunity for church families to pass on to their children the heritage of church history, family history, and mentors of peace, justice, and faith.

> On All Saint's Day each member of our family chooses a "saint." A "saint" is anyone who is exemplary in Christian faith and life—and for our purposes can be someone we know in daily life as well as a biblical or other historical figure. Because our family has a special interest in peace and peacemakers, we often choose peacemakers as our saints.
>
> On the evening of All Saint's Day, we clear the dinner table and light candles, one by one, as we share a story or anecdote about our chosen person. Then we compose a poem, which I copy on an attractive poster to display in our kitchen until the next All Saints' Day. The Halloween costumes are stuffed in the back closet, the Christmas carols and decorations are eventually tucked away in the loft, but our All Saints' Day poetry is a constant reminder of our heroes and mentors as we seek to love and serve the Lord throughout the year.
>
> The purpose of all this remembering is imitation. Hebrews 13:7 reads: ". . . consider the outcome of their way of life, and imitate their faith." Situations arise daily in the lives of our families, our churches, and our world that challenge our faith. The unrelenting prayers of my husband's grandmother; the vision of Martin Luther King, Jr.; the loving hospitality and leadership of Lydia are worthy of imitation when we are confronted with our own thorny limitations.
> —Sharon Buttry, Swedesburg, Pennsylvania[5]

---

[5]From Sharon Buttry, "What Comes After Halloween?" *Baptist Leader*, Summer 1994, 32.

A congregation can introduce this practice to the families of the church (however a family is constituted) so they can honor those who bore the faith to them and demonstrated their faith in lives of justice and peacemaking. The Baptist Peace Fellowship of North America has an excellent resource for family use on the life and witness of Martin Luther King, Jr. *Dreaming God's Dream: Family Activities Guide* contains suggested learning experiences for the whole family to explore the impact of racism and poverty and to appreciate the culture and heritage of African American people.[6] Members can be encouraged to discover a new peace-and-justice saint in church history, perhaps using a book like *Peace Be With You* by Cornelia Lehn,[7] which presents children's stories about people from church history who nonviolently stood for peace and justice or creatively loved their enemies. On the first Sunday of November, prior to the Lord's Supper, the "communion of the saints" can be recognized by asking families to name and say a brief word about one of their "saints." Hebrews 12:1-2 makes an appropriate theme text, and a sermon could be preached on a peacemaking saint.[8]

Family devotions, seasonal observances, and just plain fun can all be woven together as part of the spiritual nurture of the children. Susan Vogt is a member of the Parenting for Peace and Justice Network. Her book *Just Family Nights: 60 Activities to Keep Your Family Together in a World Falling Apart*[9] is full of family activities that include a devotional theme, educational information, or observance regarding a peace or justice theme; ways to respond to the issue; games; and even refreshment ideas.

Parents can also model their peacemaking by bringing children

---

[6]Kathleen McGinnis, *Dreaming God's Dream: Family Activities Guide*, ed. Ken Sehested. See also Ken Sehested, ed., *Dreaming God's Dream: Study Materials for Church Home and School—Learning-Based Activities for Six Age Groups*. These are available from the Baptist Peace Fellowship of North America, 499 S. Patterson, Memphis, TN 38111.

[7]Cornelia Lehn, *Peace Be With You* (Newton, Kans.: Faith and Life Press, 1980).

[8]See Paul Dekar's *For the Healing of the Nations: Baptist Peacemakers* (Macon, Ga: Smyth & Helwys Publishing, 1993) for stories from the Baptist tradition.

[9]Susan Vogt, *Just Family Nights: 60 Activities to Keep Your Family Together in a World Falling Apart* (Elgin, Ill.: Brethren Press, 1994).

with them to various peace events. If the church peacemaking group is going to a demonstration, bring the children along. (If civil disobedience actions are planned, parents should carefully consider the nature of the action, the likely police response, and whether it is appropriate or safe for children to be present.) Children can help make signs and posters. Parents should explain what is going on and why they are involved in the action. Children often can connect to the fairness issues at stake and enter enthusiastically into the event—though young ones will tire quickly! Mission work trips, especially locally, can help inculcate values of respect, service, compassion, and justice in children as they work alongside their parents and other church members.

Bible Stories and the Sunday School

Stories from the Old Testament are staples of the Sunday school curriculum, and the Old Testament is full of violence. David and Goliath can serve as a paradigm. While the lesson is that David trusted God to give him the victory, the victory came by killing the giant. Seeing this story as the paradigm for young faith places violence at the center of godly behavior, whether or not it is intentional.

Purging David and Goliath from the Sunday school curriculum isn't the answer. We need to teach these Bible stories, but the approach for the peacemaking church will need to be one of comprehensiveness and complexity. *Comprehensiveness* means that we will need to be sure to lay a foundation for faith and discipleship that is not centered on the violence of the Old Testament but on the life and call of Jesus. Jesus' work to reconcile us to God and to one another offers many stories for the teacher to unfold for the children; numerous other biblical stories also pick up these themes. *Complexity* means that as the students mature, they can grapple more and more with Scripture as well as with world issues. Juniors and teens could take the David and Goliath story and juxtapose it to the story of God's judgment when David tried to institute draft registration ("numbering the people" in 2 Samuel 24) or with Jesus' teachings of loving your enemies and turning the other cheek. How does this work out amid the conflicts they encounter at school and the options for resolving them? If young people can see movement and growth in the faith of the people in the Bible, then they can come to understand their own faith as a dynamic relationship rather than a rigid dogma handed down by their elders for them to memorize and obey.

Unfortunately, many of the church school resources produced by denominational or independent publishing houses do not deal with peace or conflict resolution—though there are a few refreshing exceptions. Christian educators who want to equip children and youth to face the conflicts and violence in their world—which for many children intrudes dramatically into their schools and neighborhoods—can write to their curriculum publishers requesting that peacemaking and conflict resolution themes be included in the development of new resources.

Creative teachers can develop their own curriculum or add peacemaking themes to standard curriculum at appropriate points. Supplemental activities can be devised or culled from some of the resource books listed in Appendix E. The Martin Luther King, Jr., curriculum published by the Baptist Peace Fellowship, *Dreaming God's Dream,* has materials ready for use in church school settings.[10] James McGinnis has put together an eleven-unit curriculum, *Educating for Peace and Justice,*[11] for grades seven through twelve. It has ideas and projects that can be used in a church school, a youth group, or as a resource to incorporate specific program pieces into a prepared program. Members of the First Baptist Church in Granville, Ohio, wanted to teach their children more extensively on peace and justice themes, so they developed their own curriculum for the entire church school.

In this age of specialization, people are unwilling to believe their own experience. Even teachers balked at creating their own curriculum; they were convinced that their experience and expertise could not be as valid as that of the "experts." It was exhilarating to see people discover their own potential, and just as exciting to see church people of every kind coming together to write a curriculum about things they believed in.

The brainstorming sessions are at the heart of the process.

---

[10] See information in footnote 6.

[11] James McGinnis, *Educating for Peace and Justice: Religious Dimensions, Grades 7-12* (St. Louis: Institute for Peace and Justice, 1993).

Helping participants delineate goals and at the same time capturing enthusiasms that can later be translated into the classroom is the role of the leader here. In this way goals are shared, excitement is generated, and tangible results are produced. It is good to try to have one professional in each small group as a resource person, but it is not necessary. Lessons can always be added to and refined later. The beauty of the process is that it acts as yeast in the congregation as a whole, not only in regard to the curriculum, but in the life of the church as well.
—Karolyn Burkett, Granville, Ohio

Vacation Bible school (VBS) programs can be a time for focused attention on the Bible and peace. The First Baptist Church of Overland Park, Kansas, set peacemaking as its congregational theme and ministry goal for 1991. That year the VBS theme of "peacemakers" was based on a curriculum developed by their minister of discipleship, Steve Edwards. Conflict resolution education for children could also be taught during VBS. Education in conflict resolution for the VBS or church school staff would help teachers deal with conflicts in their classes in a manner reflective of the values they teach. The Presbyterian Peacemaking Program developed a five-session curriculum on the theme "The Family of God: Creating a Fair Community," which is suitable either for a VBS program or church school (see Appendix B).

When the First Baptist Church of Detroit ran their VBS program in 1992, they selected the theme of Christian peacemaking.

In January 1992 the board of Christian education worked on the question "What do our children need to gain this summer from vacation Bible school?" Responses included self-esteem, learning to get along with different kinds of people in positive ways, and having fun within the context of Christian community. These answers began to reveal a common thread: Christian peacemaking. We found peacemaking to be at the heart of the gospel. Our children had great fun and learned a crucial aspect of what it means to be a disciple of Jesus at home, in the neighborhood, and at school.
—Carol McVetty, Southfield, Michigan

Once they identified peacemaking as the theme, they then set their goals: to help their children gain a sense of their own worth and the acceptance of the differences of others, learn tools for dealing with anger and resolving conflict without fighting, and develop an awareness of peacemaking as part of Christian life.

When they were unable to find curriculum to meet their needs, they created their own using some of the resources listed in Appendix E. The children were divided into small groups called "circles," named after peace heroes. They learned conflict resolution skills from the *Young Peacemakers Project Book*. Learning centers called "Shalom Shops" focused on each of the goals using different forms of activity. The VBS program culminated in planting a "peace pole" bearing the prayer "May peace prevail on earth" in the major languages spoken in their community.[12]

Preschool and After-School Programs

For churches that have preschool or after-school programs in which they have input into the curriculum, peacemaking education can be a regular part of what is done with the children. Conflict resolution curriculum and cooperative activities can be woven into the program. Many conflict resolution resources have been developed for use with children of various ages.[13] One curriculum was designed by Don DeMott of the New York Baptist Peace Fellowship. Called "Project HOPE," this curriculum has been used extensively in public schools in the state of New York in a program that has often involved church members as volunteer trainers in the public schools. The materials would be well suited for use by churches themselves in their own before- and after-school programs.[14]

The Lakeshore Avenue Baptist Church in Oakland, California, has a child-care center that provides both day care and before- and after-school care for children ages three to twelve. They decided that one way of carrying out the church's mission of reconciliation

---

[12] For a fuller description, see Carol McVetty, "Peacemaking in Vacation Bible School," *Baptist Leader*, Spring 1994, 26-27.

[13] The Lombard Mennonite Peace Center is a good clearinghouse for many resources related to peace education and conflict resolution. They can be contacted at 528 East Madison, Lombard, IL 60148 (708-627-5310).

[14] For the "Project HOPE Curriculum" contact Donald W. DeMott, 4408 East Groveland Rd., Geneseo, NY 14454.

in a diverse community was to develop a "Children's Peace Academy" to become a part of the program in their child-care center. After extensive study and testing of various programming ideas, the church launched the academy. They paid for child-care center staff to attend conflict resolution training as a staff development activity. With well-thought-out curriculum and trained staff, the children in the Lakeshore Avenue Baptist peace academy are getting an education more valuable than they can comprehend. Parents of the children are also being incorporated into the academy's program with a four-week training course on "Nurturing Young Children as Peacemakers."

There are two realities that helped keep us motivated: (1) In Oakland, as in much of the country, homicide is a leading killer of teenagers. We believed that very early intervention was part of the answer to this moral and public health crisis. (2) Howard Thurman says that there is great danger when people live in proximity but not community. We wanted to plant the seeds of respect and appreciation that later bear the fruit of community.
—Jim Hopkins, Oakland, California

A whole curriculum need not be developed or used. Many resources offer creative ideas in arts, crafts, games, and stories. Activities can be selected to weave into other programs; individual events can fill up smaller program slots. Phyllis Vos Wezeman's *Peacemaking Creatively Through the Arts*[15] is a gold mine of ideas for elementary age children, using art forms from drawing to drama to dance, from music to puppetry to mime. Cooperative games can teach ways to get along with others and to value each person's contribution to the success of the entire group. Resources in these areas are listed in Appendix E.

War Toys

Toys are often donated to church preschools and child-care centers, often with little thought to what is being given. Violent toys can be weeded out. Children often act out what they see on television with toys that are made in conjunction with children's program-

---

[15]Available from Educational Ministries, Inc., 2861-C Saturn St., Brea, CA 92621.

ming. Whether with Ninja Turtles or Power Rangers, when play turns to martial arts demonstrations, very little that is positive will result! Behavior tends to become more aggressive, selfish, and hurtful. Providing toys that are cooperative, creative, and nonviolent will channel the children's play in more constructive directions.

Toys are big business, as any parent surely knows. To toy manufacturers, children are consumers, and a huge quantity of advertising is geared toward them to whet their desires. Often lines of toys are linked to children's television shows, turning entertainment into thirty-minute advertisements. With many war toys, the children then act out the plots to the shows they have watched, complete with kicking, shooting, hitting, and other forms of violent behavior. At least half of the video games are some form of combat between people, monsters, or machines. Some games are particularly graphic in their violence, with victors beheading or ripping out internal organs of their prostrate foes.[16]

Christmas is one of the two major Christian holidays—and is certainly the one with the most glitz. For children Christmas is more about toys than the Christ child. It is tragically ironic that celebrating the birth of the Prince of Peace often entails buying war toys. That means that the peacemaking church has a good teachable moment. When the Christmas shopping season opens, the church should begin the war-toys education season.[17]

A presentation on war toys could be made in church or at a Sunday school opening program. Perhaps the youth could have a study on the issue for a few weeks and lead in the presentation. Niños y Jóvenes por la Paz de Puerto Rico (Children and Youth for Peace in Puerto Rico), a group of Baptist youth from many churches, hold annual festivals during the Christmas season to counter war toys. Some dress up as clowns, talking about war toys and distributing nonviolent toys.

---

[16]An excellent book to study the relation of toys and children's play to violence is Nancy Carlsson-Paige and Diane E. Levin, *Who's Calling the Shots? How to Respond Effectively to Children's Fascination with War Play and War Toys* (Philadelphia: New Society Publishers, 1990).

[17] The War Resisters League has a long-standing project on war toys and offers some excellent resources. For information, contact them at Children & Nonviolence Campaign, WRL, 339 Lafayette St., New York, NY 10012 (212-226-0450).

At Niños y Jóvenes por la Paz we campaign against war toys by teaching what they are and why Christians should not promote their use by our children. We learned through workshops and experience how important it is for a child to play and how much they learn while playing. That gave us ideas on how to reach kids with cooperative games, songs, and puppets. When you ask a five-year-old if killing is bad, the answer will probably be yes, but then this same kid may enjoy playing war with toy guns and soldiers.

I like to think that the kingdom of God is built brick by brick and that those bricks are made of tolerance, peace, justice, and love. When I help a young person understand that sharing will become justice and that cooperation will turn into peace, I feel that I have helped in building God's kingdom.

—Sandra Roman, Gurabo, Puerto Rico

Similar presentations could be made in church. FOR KIDS, the child advocacy ministry developed by Broadman Baptist Church in Cuyahoga Falls, Ohio, sponsored a conference entitled "Violence: Toys, Television, and Children." The conference was covered by both radio and television in the area. To encourage the use of nonviolent toys by church families, lists of constructive alternatives to giving war toys can be printed in church newsletters or bulletins.

Mission Projects for Peace Education

Kids can get very enthused about concrete projects. Their creativity and generosity can be infectious even while they learn about the world and some of its pains. With something concrete to do, they can feel empowered to make a difference. A mission project with a peacemaking theme can tap into that wellspring of enthusiasm and teach about issues and peace action.

Many children hear about wars and other calamities on the news, sometimes in conjunction with school assignments. Regular relief offerings for war-torn countries can be highlighted for the kids. In Sunday school or during the children's "sermon," ask them to say what they know about what is happening in the particular country. This will help give them a sense of participation in making a difference in something they hear about on the news.

Older children and youth can enter walk-a-thons—and some will walk three times as far as the adults as they race ahead, come back, and flit from side to side along the walk route! Teach them about the cause for which the money is being raised and invite them to raise sponsors and walk themselves.

The children from the Sunday school of the Killarney Baptist Church in Manitoba, Canada, collected one hundred thousand pennies from the churches in Killarney. This thousand dollars they raised was used to help political prisoners in Haiti who have been severely abused by political and military authorities. The project developed out of the Christian Peacemaker Teams (CPT) who had been active in Haiti. Lloyd Jersak from the church had been a part of the CPT in Haiti in 1993 and developed the idea in response to urgent appeals from the families of six prisoners.

Youth and Military Service

A big decision for many mid- to late-teens is whether or not to join the military. Teens are bombarded with recruitment ads on TV, hear recruiters at their high schools, and are often encouraged to join Junior Reserve Officer Training Corp (JROTC) programs in the public schools. Churches need to equip their youth with the ethical and biblical tools for making their own decisions about military service. Whether it takes place in a church school class or in youth group meetings, time needs to be taken to discuss the upcoming choices regarding the military and the ethics of war.

General Bible study on war and peace can be a component of the study. Adults can be involved by asking a number of church members who have had various experiences as military personnel, conscientious objectors, or peace activists to tell their stories. Youth can be asked to take one of the options (join the military, register for the draft but not join, register as a conscientious objector, or refuse to register), state the pros and cons, and argue for that particular choice.

Most denominations have a range of convictions among their members, from pacifists to people who are active members of the armed forces. Adequately equipping the youth to make their own decisions requires that they be presented the range of options and the opportunities and risks associated with each option. Overshadowing the entire decision is the question of what values one holds that determine how to weigh the options. More than funds for a college education are at stake, as members of the National Guard discovered when they were called up to go to the Persian Gulf in 1990. Many young people who had never seriously wrestled with their convictions about war and killing were caught up in a fast-moving system that did not offer them an easy way out. A congregation serves its youth well to encourage them to think through the issues before the time of crisis.

As of this writing, the selective service system and draft registration are still in place.[18] When an eighteen-year-old registers for the draft, there is no opportunity to state one's convictions as a conscientious objector (C.O.). C.O.s must wait until such time as the draft would be reinstituted. Then they have ten days from the time the draft notice is sent out to register their position with the selective service. It is important that the draftee have on record a statement of his or her convictions, particularly if not a member of a historic peace church. Some denominations have a registry for C.O.s. The teen can contact that denominational office and send a letter stating his or her convictions, which will then be kept on file in case it is needed.[19]

My decision to register myself as a conscientious objector to military service is rooted in my belief that God created us to live in harmony with God and the rest of creation. In light of this, I believe that violence is a violation of the relationship in which we are called to live, that it goes against God's intentions for us as God's children.

Even though I have made the decision to be a conscientious objector, I recognize that it is a potentially divisive issue and that there are many within the denomination who would not agree with my understanding of what our faith calls us to.

---

[18] Efforts in Congress in 1994 to close down the selective service system were defeated, though there is a possibility that this issue will be revisited. In many circles, including some sectors of the military, the draft is viewed as antiquated and ineffective for U.S. military and security needs.

[19] For American Baptists the C.O. registry is located with the Peace Program, National Ministries, P.O. Box 851, Valley Forge, PA 19482. A study packet is available entitled "War, Your Conscience and Draft Registration."

*Because of this, I believe that the denomination's willingness
to support both conscientious objectors and those who accept
military service is a powerful sign of its commitment to the soul
freedom that has always been a hallmark of Baptist faith.*
                                    —*G. Andrew Tooze, Denver, Colorado*

Study resources and information on the various dimensions of
conscientious objection are available from two major organizations: the Central Committee for Conscientious Objectors (CCCO)
and the National Interreligious Service Board for Conscientious
Objectors (NISBCO).[20] Both have produced a number of excellent
tracts on issues related to conscientious objection that help focus
the issues and provide solid information about selective service and
U.S. military procedures for C.O.s. CCCO also gathered an all-star
cast of comic-book writers to produce a comic book, "Real War
Stories." These resources provide youth with an alternative perspective to the recruiters' materials provided at taxpayer expense.

Once a person is in the military, including the National Guard, it
is very difficult to get out on grounds of conscientious objection,
particularly in the midst of a military crisis. Every person in the
National Guard is liable for call-up for full-time duty, something
that the young person considering joining needs to thoroughly
understand and evaluate. Young adults are at an age when many of
their values and convictions are being shaped and reworked; convictions are not set in stone by age eighteen! I was in ROTC in
college when I became a C.O. due to a new faith commitment. If a
person changes his or her convictions while in the military and
wants to get out, pastoral involvement can be very helpful, both as
personal support and as witness to the person's ethical development.
The pastor would need to be in touch with military officials handling
the church member's case and with counselors from NISBCO or
CCCO. Each case is different, so it is helpful to draw upon the
expertise of those who have worked the system from a variety of
angles.

Public-school programs providing military training are a concern

---

[20] The Central Committee for Conscientious Objectors is located at 2208
South St., Philadelphia, PA 19146. The National Interreligious Service Board
for Conscientious Objectors is at 1612 K St., NW, Suite 1400, Washington,
D.C. 20006-2802 (202-293-3220).

to many peace churches. JROTC programs within schools are readily accessible and present a positive view of military participation to young teens in hopes of recruiting them into the military forces following graduation. The Crest Manor Church of the Brethren in South Bend, Indiana, mobilized some other local congregations to take their concerns about JROTC to the superintendent and school board. When their proposal to drop JROTC was rejected, the churches took the issue to faculty and students, distributing fact sheets, setting up information networks, and bringing in a speaker for a special meeting. As of this writing, JROTC is still in the South Bend schools, but the churches are continuing to raise their concerns about military training as the schools are trying to deal with violence and teach conflict resolution.

Chapter 4

Christian Education: Youth and Adults

Along with the worship service, the Christian education program is the heart of the week-by-week life of the local congregation. It provides an opportunity for serious engagement with issues, both biblically and in the contemporary society. Often the setting is that of a small group, so people can participate easily in discussion and shape the program to their own interests and concerns. Topics that might be handled in only one sermon a year can be studied in depth and from a variety of angles. For the peacemaker, then, the church's Christian education program needs to be a major point of attention.

Jesus said in his Great Commission, "Go . . . teaching them to obey everything that I have commanded you" (Matthew 28:19-20). The peacemaking teachings of Jesus have often been slighted by churches for a host of reasons, from the influence of civil religion to the spiritualizing of passages that speak of peace or justice. The teachings of the Sermon on the Mount are often viewed as nice ideals that not are necessarily to be taken literally in the rough-and-tumble conflicts of the real world; loving your enemies is deemed to be impractical. As a result, major portions of what Jesus commanded are not taught as regular parts of our discipleship programs.[1]

A church executive in a war-torn country wrote me a letter about how the churches in his denomination had not taught about war and peace. "Theologically speaking we never learned or taught about the Christian responsibility on peace," he wrote. "So when the war openly started . . . there were few people and congregations reflecting or acting to face the rising problems." They were great at evangelism and personal morality, but their Christian education overlooked the social dimensions of Jesus' teaching related to violence. When the war exploded in his country, the people in most of the churches were caught off guard and without biblical grounding as to how to respond to the chaos engulfing them. As the tides of violence rise in many American communities, some of our own inadequacy in dealing with violence thoroughly and biblically is similarly being exposed.

As Christians we turn to the Scriptures for guidance; therefore, Bible study on issues of war, peace, justice, and violence can provide a solid foundation for building a responsible ethic. Then we need to bring together our biblical understanding with an analysis of the world we live in with its complexities and problems. Finally, we need to learn how to apply what we learn in practical action, becoming "doers of the word, and not merely hearers" (James 1:22). A Christian education program that can provide this kind of learning in the area of peace concerns will be well on the road to carrying out Jesus' discipling commission.

---

[1] In his book *The 100: A Ranking of the Most Influential Persons in History* (New York: Citadel Press, 1992), Michael Hart listed Jesus as number three, behind Mohammed and Isaac Newton. In explaining the reason for putting Jesus third, Hart said Jesus' most distinctive and original ethical idea was to love one's enemies, which, if it had been followed, would have moved Jesus to Hart's number-one spot: "But the truth is that they [Jesus' teachings about enemies] are not widely followed. In fact they are not even generally accepted. Most Christians consider the injunction to 'Love your enemy' as—at most—an ideal which might be realized in some perfect world, but one which is not a reasonable guide to conduct in the actual world we live in. We do not normally practice it, do not expect others to practice it. Jesus' most distinctive teaching, therefore, remains an intriguing but basically untried suggestion." Hart's assessment would make a good discussion starter for a church school class or Bible study.

Involving the Youth with the Adults

The youth in a church often have their own programs, groups, and church school classes. However, high schoolers are often very concerned about issues in the world and frequently organize to act on issues as their own convictions are developed. In the area of peacemaking in particular, youth have as much a stake as adults in what happens, if not more. They are nearing the age when they could enter into the military, and they can see the state of the world they will inherit from adults. Programming related specifically to youth is good, but it is also important to begin integrating what the youth are learning and doing into the life of the full community of faith.

The churches in Puerto Rico have a model regarding youth ministry that might be helpful to U.S. churches. They define youth as roughly from fifteen to thirty years of age. They have youth organizations, including peace groups, that are self-governing, and they organize programs for their members and outreach activities into the churches and wider community. The typical U.S. division between youth and adults at about age eighteen (or high school graduation) groups older teens with children, with a clear deline-ation between them and adults. The Puerto Rican churches have their older teens working with young adults in situations where they can take full responsibility for what they do. The young adults are also in leadership positions rather than on the sidelines of churches (in which the leadership roles are taken by older members who have been around a long time). People can graduate from seminary and become pastors while still being "youth." Both teens and young adults, in this definition of youth, can stretch toward using their gifts and developing their leadership capability, which is probably a major contributing factor to the high level of capable young lead-ership in the Puerto Rican churches.

Changing the definition of youth may not be culturally feasible, but a congregation can make an intentional effort to involve older teens as full participants in the peacemaking education and action of the church. The classes that study the Bible or social issues can be done by youth groups as well as adult groups—and they can also be mixed. The mixing probably won't occur without direct and persistent invitations to the young people, and then a repeated effort to communicate their importance to the group by involving them fully in the study and discussion. Youth should be invited to serve on planning committees for peacemaking ministry, and their ideas should be actively solicited and incorporated into the church's peacemaking program.

Education can also take place through modeling—living out peacemaking in action with the youth. Every December there is a peace pilgrimage from Nazareth to Bethlehem, Pennsylvania. The ten-mile walk culminates in an ecumenical service with a noted peacemaker speaking. Members of the Royersford Baptist Church, including the youth group, often participate. To share conversation in the long walk and to take in the content presented by the speaker at the closing service gives youth an opportunity to learn as they act in partnership with the adults in the congregation.

> *As it became obvious that President Bush planned to commit U.S. troops to the Persian Gulf, increasing numbers of people in my congregation asked what they could do to "wage peace." On the day before the fighting actually started, thirty-five people from our church drove to Washington to urge our members of Congress to seek nonviolent solutions to the conflict. After a briefing at the American Baptist Churches' Office of Governmental Relations, we divided the group into four delegations to visit the offices of four separate members of Congress. Ten of the thirty-five people were middle- and senior-high-school youth who had taken a day off school to be with us. The youth were encouraged to comment or ask questions if they wanted to; but whether they spoke or not, it was undoubtedly one of the most important days in their lives as they were given the means for acting on their beliefs.*
> —Martin Massaglia, Royersford, Pennsylvania

Most of the activities outlined in this book can be done by youth as well as adults, and their involvement together begins by respecting the integrity of the youth as disciples of Christ.

Classes Studying Peace

The backbone of many Christian education programs is the church school. Bible study groups, either in homes or at the church building, also provide a major setting for Christian education. These classes and groups are prime places for studying peacemaking from a biblical basis. Unfortunately there is much biblical illiteracy on matters of peace and justice; the wealth of biblical material will keep a class going for a long time.

One form of Bible study is simply to dig into the Bible, using a concordance to do a study of peace-related passages. *A Bible Study Guide: War and Peace* and *A Bible Study Guide on Conflict Resolution* are workbooks I've put together to provide Bible texts and questions to help class participants expand their own understanding of what the passages say.[2]

A few years ago I used the Bible Study Guide: War and Peace with the adult Sunday school class I was teaching at that time. This group of young adults plunged into the challenge of pursuing the threads of war and peace through Scripture with enthusiasm and a healthy skepticism about what anybody else was going to tell them the Bible said. However, they really appreciated the starting point of the study, Jesus' teaching about war and peace, rather than a strictly table-of-contents linear approach. They found that anchored the whole study. My class had a great time using it.
—Carol Franklin Sutton, Norristown, Pennsylvania

The Presbyterian Peacemaking Program has a series of excellent Bible studies on peace themes in Genesis, the Psalms, Isaiah, Jeremiah, Luke, Acts, and the Corinthian letters.[3] These studies in a particular biblical book examine selected passages with contemporary vignettes to provoke discussion about current implications of the biblical teaching. The Kerygma Program also has a series of Bible studies on many topics, including one on peace entitled *Shalom*.[4]

A variety of books have been written about the peacemaking teachings of the Bible. One could be selected for class use, with everyone reading a chapter a week and discussing the material.

---

[2] These guides are available from National Ministries Literature Resources, P.O. Box 851, Valley Forge, PA 19482. The war and peace study guide is also available in Spanish and is called *Guía de Estudio Bíblico: Guerra y Paz*.

[3] These can be obtained through the Presbyterian Peacemaking Program, 100 Witherspoon St., Louisville, KY 40202-1396.

[4] For information, contact the Kerygma Program, 300 Mt. Lebanon Blvd., Suite 205, Pittsburgh, PA 15234 (800-KERYGMA).

Richard McSorley's *New Testament Basis of Peacemaking*[5] provides an overview of the New Testament from the point of a Catholic pacifist. Walter Wink's *Violence and Nonviolence in South Africa: Jesus' Third Way*[6] examines the Sermon on the Mount in the challenging contexts of biblical Palestine and apartheid-era South Africa. In *The Way God Fights,*[7] Lois Barrett examines the Old Testament war stories from a peace perspective and offers some interesting insights. *Christ and Violence* by Ron Sider[8] looks at the New Testament teachings by and about Jesus along the thematic lines related to violence issues. Robert McAfee Brown helps readers step into the context of the poor nations to hear the Bible's liberation perspective anew in his book *Unexpected News: Reading the Bible with Third World Eyes.*[9] For classes that are confident about taking on more difficult topics, *Ain't Gonna Study War No More* by Albert Curry Winn[10] directly deals with the ambiguities in the Bible regarding war and peace and the variety of traditions all taught within Scripture. William Herzog gives some surprising and illuminating interpretations of the parables of Jesus in *Parables as Subversive Speech: Jesus as Pedagogue of the Oppressed.*[11] My book *Christian Peacemaking: From Heritage to Hope*[12] includes two chapters on biblical material related to nonviolent action and conflict resolution. (Our books through your local Christian bookstore.)

A different approach could be to discuss the various positions

---

[5]Richard McSorley, *New Testament Basis of Peacemaking* (Scottdale, Pa.: Herald Press, 1979).

[6]Walter Wink, *Violence and Nonviolence in South Africa: Jesus' Third Way* (Philadelphia: New Society Publishers, 1987).

[7] Lois Barrett, *The Way God Fights: War and Peace in the Old Testament* (Scottdale, Pa.: Herald Press, 1987).

[8] Ronald J. Sider, *Christ and Violence* (Scottdale, Pa.: Herald Press, 1979).

[9] Robert McAfee Brown, *Unexpected News: Reading the Bible with Third World Eyes* (Philadelphia: Westminster Press, 1984).

[10]Albert Curry Winn, *Ain't Gonna Study War No More* (Louisville, Ky.: Westminster/John Knox Press, 1993).

[11] William R. Herzog II, *Parables as Subversive Speech: Jesus as Pedagogue of the Oppressed* (Louisville, Ky.: Westminster/John Knox Press, 1994).

[12]Daniel Buttry, *Christian Peacemaking: From Heritage to Hope* (Valley Forge, Pa.: Judson Press, 1994).

taken on war and peace by Christians. *War: Four Christian Views*[13] has four presentations on nonresistance, Christian pacifism, just war, and the crusade or preventative war by proponents of those views, followed by responses from the other contributors. Roland Bainton's classic *Christian Attitudes Toward War and Peace*[14] provides a historical overview of the development of the basic Christian traditions regarding war. Both these books, however, are missing the recent contributions of liberation theology to this issue. To get a range of liberationist perspectives related to the question of war and nonviolence, a class could read together *Theology and Violence: The South African Debate.*[15]

Many other books related to current conflict areas or peace issues could be studied by groups. A number of good books are available through the book services of Sojourners and the Fellowship of Reconciliation (see their addresses in Appendix B). Browsing through a Christian bookstore, unfortunately, will provide only a very limited selection of books related to peace concerns. You may even find more titles taking a militaristic approach to conflicts and U.S. policy. Titles you see reviewed in magazines and journals usually can be ordered by local bookstores, however. While ordering, encourage the bookstore to stock more titles in the area of peacemaking concerns—and then shop there to encourage its continued stocking of a broader selection of books on social issues.

Other Educational Settings

Besides classes and Bible studies, peace education in the church can take place in a wide variety of settings. Speakers can be brought in during the church school hour, for presentations following the worship service, or for special events during the week or weekend. If someone from another church or from your community has traveled to a conflicted zone or an "enemy" country, invite that person to come and tell his or her stories. Invite missionaries

---

[13] Robert G. Clouse, ed., *War: Four Christian Views* (Downers Grove, Ill.: Intervarsity Press, 1981).

[14] Roland H. Bainton, *Christian Attitudes Toward War and Peace* (Nashville: Abingdon Press, 1960).

[15] Charles Villa-Vicencio, ed., *Theology and Violence: The South African Debate* (Grand Rapids: Wm. B. Eerdmans, 1988).

working in conflicted countries to come discuss what is happening and tell of the ministries going on in the midst of the violence. Peace activists can come to address pressing issues on the national agenda. During the height of the war in El Salvador, many refugees staying in sanctuary churches went to neighboring congregations to relate their experiences.

For some issues, a special forum can be set up to allow a diversity of opinions or a variety of approaches to be presented. If a church is concerned about not taking sides on a particular matter, a forum will allow the issue to at least be discussed. Advocates from a number of points of view can state their cases, and members of the congregation can shape their own opinions— and probably everyone will hear perspectives they may not have heard before.

The Study Circles Resource Center has stimulated the growth of small groups studying current issues, including many peace concerns.[16] The groups are set up for limited periods of time, usually four to five weeks. A group could meet at a church, in someone's home, or during lunch hour at a central location in a business district. The discussion guides available from the resource center are very inexpensive and are focused on timely issues. A congregation could use them for their own exploration of issues or as part of an outreach program to the community to stimulate ethical thinking about concerns on the national agenda.

Simulation games can provide fun as well as a stimulating educational experience. Usually twenty to forty people are needed to successfully play such a game. The games may take up to two hours to play, plus time to debrief. They are often specific to a particular era or peace issue, so they may become dated or discontinued by the organization that developed them. Keeping an eye on resource listings in social concerns magazines or peace organization newsletters will let you know when new games are available.[17]

---

[16] For information contact the Study Circles Resource Center, Route 169, P.O. Box 203, Pomfret, CT 06258 (203-928-2616).

[17] The Office of Governmental Relations for the American Baptist Churches has developed a simulation game on the shaping of the U.S. budget, including military spending. "Paths to Power: How the Federal Budget Reflects Power" is available from National Ministries Literature Resources, P.O. Box 851, Valley Forge, PA 19482-0851.

Simulation games can be played at a retreat, as part of a weekend afternoon special event, or at an evening gathering. Debriefing time is very important, as discussing what happened makes explicit the learnings as well as provides an opportunity to compare the events in the game with the events in real life. Simulation games are also an excellent way for youth and adults to participate together as equals in an educational experience.

Videos are a widely available educational tool. Many peace videos can be obtained through peace organizations, though central lending or distribution sources are hard to find. EcuFilm has videos for participating denominations.[18] A nonreligious source for purchase of reasonably priced videos on peace and ecological issues is the Video Project.[19] Many denominations have their own film libraries, which can be contacted to obtain the peace listings.

A video can be shown in a class or as part of a larger educational event. Always preview the video so you will know the content and how appropriate it is to what you are trying to do—and to be sure the tape is in good shape and your equipment works. Discussion following the showing of the video helps crystalize the learnings, focuses questions and disagreements, and lets the leader introduce action steps people can take in response. Commercial films available through neighborhood video stores, such as *Romero* and *The Mission,* can contribute to good learning experiences, though they tend to be too long for most program settings, and some movies may not be appropriate for younger viewers.

Sometimes education can be woven together with action. The First Baptist Church in Norristown, Pennsylvania, wove together environmental and justice concerns during an Earth Day celebration. With the help of a Native American member of the congregation, the youth fellowship presented a program that linked environmental concerns with the issue of Indian treaty rights, which was exploding into violence over Chippewa spearfishing in northern Wisconsin. After a videotape was shown, the church members rallied outside with treaty support posters.

---

[18] Contact EcuFilm at 810 Twelfth Ave., South, Nashville, TN 39203 (800-251-4091).

[19] Contact the Video Project at 5332 College Ave., Suite 101, Oakland, CA 94618.

As a person of Native American ancestry, I have been involved in Indian rights issues for many years. I have also been a Christian for many years and just as involved in the life of my church. When heated conflicts erupted over fishing rights in Wisconsin, Washington, and Alaska, I appealed to my church for support. However, since there had been little or no information about the violence directed toward the Indian population in these areas, it was necessary to educate the congregation. An Earth Day celebration seemed the logical platform to present the issues and survey effective advocacy procedures. The pictures that were taken, along with an accompanying article, were sent to Indian newspapers and were subsequently published.

The event sparked a sense of social justice among our young people as they expressed an eagerness to pursue solutions. It was a gratifying and affirming experience for me to share the concerns of my heart within the walls of the church. Issues of justice belong in the church, which is, after all, the body of Christ, and I believe he demands it. Mission work is as important to the life of the church as its banquets and bazaars. Although the dominant concept of "missions" is packaging mittens or blankets in a box to send to a far-away land, Indian issues are usually political in nature and require distinctive and sophisticated action, which may be as simple as writing letters to our legislators but sends a signal that the church abides by higher laws: "Love thy neighbor as thyself."

—Sandra Cianciulli, Norristown, Pennsylvania

The Church Library

Many church libraries are collections of old books stuck off in a forgotten corner of the church. They are relics of by-gone days when the church was the center of social life. With a little work, a church library can become an important ingredient in the congregation's Christian education program. Bring the library into the heavily trafficked areas of the church, such as next to the church office, in the fellowship hall, or wherever people gather before or after church. Make an inviting space for people to sit and relax. Display new selections and magazines and newsletters, and keep changing the displays so that there is always something new and interesting to see. The library for the Broadway Baptist Church in Fort Worth, Texas, is a bright room opposite the main entrance to the building.

There are plenty of chairs to sit in, and an inviting atmosphere draws in both members and visitors.

A library can also be incorporated into a multipurpose project. The Emmanuel Baptist Church in Ridgewood, New Jersey, honored two of its peacemaking members by creating a "peace lounge" as a quiet place for reading and meditation. The lounge houses a collection of literature on pacifism and a painting of Jesus as Prince of Peace. It is also available for special lectures and discussions.

Purchase some of the books listed in the bibliographies in Appendix D for your library. Invite individuals to donate from their own personal libraries; if they have read a book, they can pass on the wealth by donating it to the church library. Subscriptions to Christian peace-and-justice magazines and newsletters from peace organizations will provide the library updated material that can be prominently displayed and reach people who may not be aware that such publications even exist. Members of the congregation can buy gift subscriptions to Christian peace-and-justice periodicals for the library as a sign of support.

Develop a children's section, including titles listed in Appendix E. A story time could be held in the library during the coffee hour. Encourage teachers and students of church school classes as well as day-care or after-school programs to use your library facilities and familiarize themselves with what is available. Teachers' and parents' resources can be collected and clearly displayed.

If you are going to make your library a valuable resource, you'll need to publicize it again and again. Make announcements about new resources being located there. Have people write book reviews in the church newsletter. A library is of value only if people use the resources in it, and people will use them only if they know what is there and that it will help them.

Peace Education and the College Town Church

When a church is located near a college or university, opportunities in peace education can benefit both the church and the college community. Students will often visit and become regular attenders, especially if a congregation is intentional about incorporating students into its church life. Professors and administrative staff may be members of the church, providing an intimate link between the religious and educational institutions. With a little thought and diligence, this relationship can strengthen the peace education component of a church's Christian education program.

The church can structure some of its educational program to coincide with the college's academic schedule, allowing students to participate as full members of a class or group studying a peace topic. Notices of the educational offerings of the church can be posted or listed in appropriate newspapers so that students will be aware of what is going on and know that they are particularly welcome. When a special event is being held that has contemporary significance—such as a missionary speaker from a war zone or a delegate from a friendship tour giving a report—the program can be publicized on campus.

Contact the leadership of campus ministry groups to let them know about your church and the programs you have. Some groups may not be interested in peace matters, but offer to provide special programming such as a Bible study on peace or a report on reconciliation work by Christians in a war-torn country. Members or leaders of the campus ministry groups could be invited to join church members who go on a friendship tour or mission work group.

If the college or university has a chaplain, let him or her know of your interest in the students and willingness to assist in showing students at a local level how Christians seek to respond to contemporary issues. A chaplain might be delighted to have a pastor or peace group leader come to speak to a student group.

On the wall in our living room is a poster an Oberlin College student gave us on his return from a trip to Central America. This student never attended our church but began to consider himself an "awakened Christian" because of our contact with him through the Central America Task Force, a student-led group. We have learned that if you are going to be involved in peace-and-justice ministry at a college or university, you need to be on campus as much as you can be, listening to the concerns being expressed and linking with people on campus who are actively exploring and working on peace-and-justice concerns. You can learn about what's going on by reading the campus newspaper, looking at the posters around campus, attending special programs and lectures, and by simply talking to the students, faculty, and staff you already know.

If there is a demonstration or program on campus dealing with some peace-and-justice concern, we get as involved as possible because it is important to be very public on campus in your commitment to such issues. The presence of clergy and other church folk at such events bears witness to the Christian and non-Christian campus communities, and that public presence can lead to a variety of private conversations. In our ministry at Oberlin, we try to "work both ends against the middle"; that is, we try to help Christians understand the importance of many of these peace-and-justice concerns to the gospel, while helping those who approach these issues from a secular perspective realize that there are religious motivations for become involved in peace-and-justice work. Both groups need to hear you talking about the Bible.

—Stephen and Mary Hammond, Oberlin, Ohio

The college is also a rich resource for the church to enjoy. Be sure the church is on the publicity list for special events on campus. When speakers visit who will address a matter on the peace agenda, publicize the event at church or organize a group to go together from the church. Professors can also be invited to participate on panels for peace education events at the church, providing historical, social, or economic background to the particular issue the church is addressing. Courses in current affairs, the Middle East, third-world politics, or liberation theology may be open for members of the community to audit or take for credit. Then the church member who takes the course could make a report to an adult church school class or peacemaker group about the new learnings gained.

Adult education can always go on as we explore more about the world and the amazing complexity and challenges of human community. Educating for peacemaking will put the church members at the growing point where faith and everyday life meet. The result will be tougher questions, a more dynamic faith, and a deeper engagement with the issues of the day.

Chapter 5

Evangelism and Peacemaking

For some people, linking evangelism and peacemaking seems like mixing apples and oranges or, worse yet, poison and fruit. One side may be fixed on stereotypes of evangelists as fundamentalist militarists calling people to Jesus while cheering the preparations for Armageddon. The other side may view peacemakers as long-haired anarchists with communist tendencies or wishy-washy liberal humanists who don't know Jesus. Of course, few people fit those stereotypes. When we dialogue with people who are different from us theologically or politically about who we are and what we believe, we find many nuances of thought that belie stereotypes and give a far more complex picture of people than will fit into nice, simplistic categories.

People may have different definitions of what *evangelism* means. We will use the term's most common meaning: calling people to a faith commitment in Jesus Christ. Evangelism and peacemaking are woven together in the same message. In fact, a strong case can be made that the fully evangelical church is a peacemaking church and that full peacemaking is evangelistic.

The Gospel of Peace

In its description of the armor of God, Ephesians 6:15 exhorts us, "As shoes for your feet put on whatever will make you ready to proclaim the gospel of peace." The gospel message is one of peace, from the angels heralding "on earth peace" at the birth of Jesus to the final triumph of God's future when "nation shall not lift up sword against nation, neither shall they learn war anymore" (Luke 2:14; Isaiah 2:4). The apostle Paul used the word *reconciliation* frequently in his writings. In Romans 5 he writes about the peace with God that we have as a result of the reconciling work of Christ on the cross. We who were enemies were reconciled by Christ's death. But that vertical peace has a horizontal dimension that Paul clearly spells out in Romans 12 when he speaks about living peaceably with all people, not taking vengeance, feeding your hungry enemies, and overcoming evil with good. The same dual reconciliation between God and people and between various people is found in 2 Corinthians 5 and Ephesians 2. The gospel that calls us to be reconciled to God inherently works for interpersonal peace.

The cross, in particular, is spoken of as an agent of peace. Christ's death reconciles us to God. It also is the force that breaks down the walls dividing people from one another, according to Ephesians 2. The crucified Jesus becomes *"our* peace" (Ephesians 2:14, italics mine). To proclaim the cross of Christ without the claim of being reconciled to other people is to proclaim what Dietrich Bonhoeffer called "cheap grace." It is evangelism without discipleship—and therefore not the kind of evangelism spoken of in the New Testament. Every person who responded to the call of Jesus to follow had to leave something behind. To respond to the gospel requires that the enmity, bitterness, fear, and prejudice that divide us from others and fuel the conflicts between us be laid aside.

The gospel of peace calls people into a new peoplehood beyond the divisiveness that draws up the battle lines. The Jew/Gentile distinction was the point of difficulty for the early church through which they learned that Christ was their peace, making the two one. As Paul said in Galatians 3:28, "There is no longer Jew or Greek, there is no longer slave or free, there is no longer male and female; for all of you are one in Christ Jesus." This unity transcending human diversity is reflected in the vision in Revelation 7:9 of the great multitude of people "from every nation, from all tribes and peoples and languages." Evangelism doesn't just call individuals to get their "souls saved." It calls us to be the new people of God, which means racial, social, and national exclusiveness must be left behind.

Evangelistic Services

When a church is involved in evangelistic services or a regular worship service with an evangelistic theme, people are being called to make commitments to Christ. Peacemaking can be woven explicitly into that call to commitment. Some of the sins from which we turn away include racism, hatred of enemies, and the desire to "get even." The call to follow Jesus includes being willing to love our enemies, forgive those who persecute us, going to the one with whom our relationships are broken, and becoming reconciled. The sins from which we are saved are not just personal but also social dynamics and structures of injustice. We are freed to become builders with Christ of the reign of God on earth as it is in heaven.

There are some peacemaking evangelists who can call people to faith in Christ in a thoroughgoing commitment that encompasses both personal and global peacemaking. Ken Sehested, Myron Augsburger, Tony Campolo, Karen Burton Mains, and Ron Sider are among those who have long records of evangelistic peacemaking or peace-filled evangelism. A local church could invite such a speaker to lead in a series of evangelistic meetings or spiritual-emphasis week. (Peacemakers should steer clear of the word *crusade* because it harks back to some of the bloodiest crimes in history committed in the name of God. Evangelism among Muslims is still greatly hindered by the memory of Christian Crusaders.)

When Kyle Childress was a new pastor at Mt. Pleasant Baptist Church in Franklin, Texas, he invited Ken Sehested of the Baptist Peace Fellowship to lead a series of evangelistic meetings.

The first night of the revival meeting half of the congregation boycotted the worship service because they thought Ken was an "outsider" who was preaching "politics" instead of "salvation." After the first night of hearing him preach, however, word spread that Ken was a fellow Texan who preached a strong biblical message. At the same time, Ken personally visited the leaders of the boycott and convinced them to change their minds. The rest of the week the services were packed.
—Kyle Childress, Nacogdoches, Texas

The call to commitment to Christ can challenge some fundamental loyalties in a person's life because of the peacemaking dimension of discipleship. At the end of the first Urban Peace and Justice Summit in Kansas City in 1993, Charles Mac Jones preached an evangelistic message to the gang members who had gathered to talk about peace. He preached about the prodigal children mired in "hog pen mentality" in which we violate one another. He talked about the welcoming party of the God who eagerly awaits us to come home from the hog pen. Then he gave the invitation, calling for the gang members to lay down their "colors," the sign of their gang affiliation, and work for unity, justice, and peace.[1] When some young men came forward and laid their colored "rags" at the altar, it was clear that a profound commitment was being made.

But the same kind of challenge can be made by the gospel to people in socially acceptable professions. I was approached by a young man who was a technician at a company making guidance systems for nuclear missiles. He realized that Christ's call to discipleship was incompatible with his job. If he was going to follow Jesus, how could he make weapons of mass destruction? Like the rich young ruler, he was challenged by Christ's claims, claims that were very difficult to swallow. After much soul-searching, the courageous young man decided to leave his new career and the security it offered. His response to the gospel cost him his job because of the connection between the gospel and peace.

The Sojourners community in Washington has sponsored "revival services" on the theme "Let Justice Roll Down." Its founder, Jim Wallis, preaches, and Christian performer/composer Ken Medema sings. Usually congregations in a metro area have joined together to sponsor the revival, which calls people to faith in Christ through a comprehensive commitment addressing the issues of justice and peace. A similar type of "revival" can be organized using local peacemaking pastors and musical groups. Denominational peace offices or regional peace fellowship groups are good sources for possible preachers and musicians in your area that can combine peace and evangelism.

The life of John Newton illustrates the importance of both

---

[1]Charles Mac Jones, "Finding Ourselves at Last," *Sojourners*, August 1993, 28-30.

evangelism and peacemaking—or in his case, more specifically, justice making. John Newton is celebrated for writing "Amazing Grace," along with many other hymns. Many people know of his life as a slaveship captain and celebrate God redeeming him out of such a sinful profession and leading him into the ministry. But it is seldom told that the same "amazing grace" that "saved a wretch like me" also compelled him to not just leave slaving but to become an activist for its abolishment. He wrote antislavery tracts and was a major influence on William Wilberforce's becoming an abolitionist leader. Newton is much like Zacchaeus, a person whose encounter with the gospel required a radical social reorientation toward justice. Conversion stories like these tell not only the happy endings but also the challenging endings. Giving hearers examples such as Zacchaeus and John Newton will help them count the cost for following Jesus, something Jesus himself did in his evangelistic invitations (Luke 14:25-33).

Peace Begins with Me

A church that is highly active in peacemaking ventures needs to be sure to periodically take time to have people look inward at their own commitments. Peace begins within. Peace activists can operate out of guilt or fear; they can be "activists" because it is easier to deal with issues "out there" than to face their own inner needs or broken intimate relationships. Anger is a powerful engine for action, whether direct anger at an injustice or transferred anger from one's past aimed at authority figures. But anger alone in a human heart becomes corrosive and hateful. Some people work diligently for peace but do not know peace in their own selves.

By calling peace activists and all the members of a congregation to a new or fuller commitment to Christ, there can be a liberating and peace-filling experience of God's grace. If we know we are loved by God, we can be free to look honestly at the places within ourselves where conflict is generated. We can release the hurt and anger of our injuries to the Christ who bears all, allowing us to forgive those who have treated us unjustly. Knowing we have been loved enables us to look at our enemies through the loving eyes of Christ, giving us the strength and resolve to be reconciled.

At times conflict can be so severe that all hope vanishes. A peace church persists in proclaiming a gospel of hope. During the most tense days of the Cold War, it was clear that humanity had the capability of self-extinction through a nuclear holocaust. Many activists were filled with despair as they painted horrifying pictures of what an atomic bomb would do to their cities. Their concerns needed to be taken seriously, for the perils were—and still are— genuine. But there was a need for good news, for a message of hope. A church that was involved in working for peace could carry the message with them that God was actively involved in human affairs. The One who made the world is in the process of redeeming it. Christ has shown we are not alone, adrift in the cosmos. Emmanuel, "God with us," has come, entered into our suffering, and triumphed over death. An activist's commitment is not taken away but is rather energized by a living hope that what we do is not in vain. I have had opportunities on the picket line to share "the hope that is in" me (see 1 Peter 3:15) with dedicated, caring peace activists who felt despair before the bomb or government intransigence.

For peace to be forged between people or nations, individuals must change. A cessation of hostilities may result because of fatigue from the fighting or a pragmatic assessment of the situation, but for peace to take place, matters of the heart, such as forgiveness, must be involved. Evangelism brings people to the God who can change the heart, thus making peace possible. Much more needs to take place than just asking Jesus to come into one's life if a person is to become a responsible disciple in the middle of a conflicted world. But with God at work within a person, forgiveness can be un- leashed, enemies can be seen with new eyes, arrogance can be replaced with humility, fear can be transformed into courage, and hope can give the sustaining energy to persevere.

Chapter 6

Peacemaking through the Arts

The Psalms exhort us to praise God in many different art forms, including music and dance. Art can be a peacemaking ministry. It can reveal truth with a directness and power that words cannot convey. Art can move us at the core of our being, energizing action on peace and justice. The arts can help us cry, express our rage, give birth to hope, and be fountains for our joy. As peacemakers we should never be so serious that we neglect the arts—or perhaps we should be so serious in our work that we give significant attention to the arts.

Music

Music is a major artistic field, and it has been covered to some extent in the chapter on worship. Music is the art form with which churches seem most familiar and comfortable. But music also can be used as congregational peacemakers move out of the sanctuary. Hymns can take on new meaning when put in the context of struggles for justice and peace. The civil rights movement marched to freedom songs born in the church. Singing about Paul and Silas being in jail made the ancient biblical stories a powerful inspiration as protesters were hauled off to their own jail cells for challenging the segregation laws. Music can flow from the sanctuary to the streets to the courthouse and jailhouse.

During the United Nations's Third Special Session on Disarmament, Darrell Adams sang at a prayer vigil under the Isaiah Wall. E. A. Hoffman's hymn, "Leaning On the Everlasting Arms," was filled with new meaning as leaders from around the world were discussing how to curb the threat of nuclear weaponry:

What have I to dread, what have I to fear,
Leaning on the everlasting arms?
I have blessed peace with my Lord so near,
Leaning on the everlasting arms.
Leaning on Jesus, leaning on Jesus,
Safe and secure from all alarms;
Leaning on Jesus, leaning on Jesus,
Leaning on the everlasting arms.

Darrell made a prophetic statement of ultimate trust that deeply stirred old Baptist pietistic hearts.

Music has also been used as a bridge builder. As musical groups from the Soviet Union, Cuba, and other "enemy" countries have toured in U.S. churches, people have been able to see the "enemy," connect at a common point of human experience, and be found together in a shared faith across language and national barriers. Churches who have hosted such musical tours have used the occasion to educate the congregation and the wider community about the conflict and the efforts of bridge-building.

One of our peacemakers on a trip to visit Christians in the old Soviet Union was an African American woman, Lemuel Buttler, from New York City. We soon learned that she loved to sing, especially the songs from her heritage. We could not have planned what transpired. In church after church, her music bridged the gap between very different cultures. Americans and Russians alike found ourselves in the arms of the God of Peace as she sang the songs of suffering from her people's heritage.

On another trip five years later, one of the Native American Indians in our party, Reaves Nahwooks, sang Comanche hymns in Romania, Hungary, and all the way to the International Baptist Peace Conference in Sweden. Once more we were drawn in the embrace of the God of Peace. Music is a language beyond language.

—Richard Myers, West Henrietta, New York

Music concerts can also be held with peace-and-justice themes. Some churches have hosted Sojourners's "Let Justice Roll Down" revivals with peacemaker Jim Wallis preaching and gifted Christian musician Ken Medema doing the music.[1] Some congregations have formed music groups to minister in the congregation, in conferences, and in the streets. "Just Us" came out of the University Baptist Church in Seattle; "Harmony and Struggle" from First Baptist in Granville, Ohio; and "The String Bean Band" out of Providence Baptist Church in Stoneville, North Carolina. Churches without such musical talent can invite nearby groups or solo artists to put on a program that will stretch the congregation's perspective to embrace concerns for justice and peace in the world. Concerts serve as energizing fund-raisers for peacemaking projects. Thousands of dollars in scholarship assistance was raised for the International Baptist Peace Conference in Nicaragua in 1992 through benefit concerts at local churches.

The Visual Arts

In many sanctuaries banners add color and lift spirits of worshipers. Banners can be made on peace themes, sometimes tailored to the specific season ("Peace on Earth" at Christmas, "Breaking Down the Dividing Wall of Hostility" during Lent). Banners provide a graphic witness when a group from the church is participating in community programs or in demonstrations. The banner identifies the church's presence and lifts up particular Christian themes in peacemaking. The Central Baptist Church in Wayne, Pennsylvania, has made banners of all the various groups and ministries in their church, including a number of peacemaking ministries. These banners are displayed in their multipurpose room as a constant reminder of the various callings and activities within the congregation. On one Peace Sunday the First Baptist Church of Waltham, Massachusetts, used a pulpit cloth and wall hangings made by the children to celebrate peace.

Our church's vision of becoming a community in which the multicultural nature of God's kingdom can be seen and experienced is in the early stages of being realized. We are experi-

---

[1]For information, contact Sojourners at address in Appendix B.

*menting in a number of areas, feeling our way along by "trial
and error." Our worship committee has created six-piece sets
of banners that hang along the outside aisles of our sanctuary.
The banners give visual messages that are racially inclusive. A
set of "Angel Banners" depicts angels with various skin tones.
A set of "Pentecost Banners" proclaims "Jesus is Lord" in six
languages accompanied by ethnically diverse human figures.
A mini art gallery is being developed in a prominent area of the
church building to display ethnic depictions of Jesus Christ.*
                              —Reid Trulson, Wauwatosa, Wisconsin

Paintings that speak to peace-and-justice themes flowing out of
the Bible or a church's history both educate and inspire. Second
Baptist Church in Detroit was in the forefront of the struggle to
emancipate slaves and achieve justice for African Americans. The
church served as the last station on the Underground Railroad
before escaped slaves reached Canada. In the church's fellowship
hall they have hung paintings detailing their history, especially their
pioneering in the quest for freedom and justice.

*Art, portrayals in painting, is indeed the highest form of
flattery since it is the result of painstaking effort and ability in
comparison to snapshot picture taking. At Second Baptist we
have witnessed creative art in which the painter made history
visible from an idea. The first is a series of paintings by a
sixteen-year-old to represent our humble yet determined beginnings before Michigan received statehood. The most significant
is a twenty-four-footer "Christ Weeping Over Detroit"—a sermon on the wall (based on Luke 19:41).*
                              —Nathaniel Leach, Detroit, Michigan

Art shows can be held, perhaps inviting community artists or
children in the church to display their work. An art contest for
children could be held with an appropriate prize, such as a "hugga-
ble planet" pillow, awarded for leading entries.

*The pen may be mightier than the sword, but you may be
surprised at the power in a Crayola! A third grader's crayoned
vision of a strife-free world has the power to make adults shake
their heads and feel a greater resolve to work for peace. Ninety
pieces of art magnify the effect!*
Children in our community have had an opportunity to share

their ideas about peace in an annual art show held at our church, a metropolitan congregation on the fringe of the inner city. The "Peace by Peace Art Show" has evolved over a five-year period.[2] Each year it is a bit different, but the primary purpose has been the same: to provide a vehicle for children in grades one through six to share their ideas on how to have peace in homes, neighborhoods, and the world.

The event has been well received by church and community and has had some serendipitous spin-offs (an eight-year-old's drawing became cover art for a national magazine associated with our denomination). This show affirmed and reinforced children's ideas on nonviolence in their world. The event has also given our church's Christian witness for peace a higher profile in the community. Many people entered our doors for the first time to view a work by their child or pupil.

—Jane Grant, Rochester, New York

Urban churches can use the mural art form that has transformed drab brick or concrete walls into vibrant expressions of life. The First Baptist Church in Los Angeles has a large wall along its parking lot. Concerned that the walls would become targets for local graffiti artists, church members turned it into a "Street Gallery" by inviting teenage artists in their neighborhood youth program to paint a series of murals.

The paintings were products of the imaginations of the kids. No direction was given other than that the paintings should express goodwill, brotherhood, and so on. One I thought most profound was of bombs coming from a plane in the sky. As they were falling, the noses of the bombs burst into bouquets of flowers.

The murals lasted quite a while. They finally deteriorated and were painted over. There was a lot of interest in the congregation. The results were quite good for amateurs. It was also quite a testimony to the neighborhood.

—John Townsend, Los Angeles, California

---

[2] The original inspiration for the "Peace by Peace Art Show" came from the "World at Peace Art Show" sponsored by the Pullen Memorial Baptist Church. Pullen Memorial will provide information for those wishing to sponsor their own art show. Write Pullen Memorial Baptist Church at 1801 Hillsborough St., Raleigh, NC 27605.

Public art is a good way to make a life- and peace-affirming statement to the community and to make the presence of the church known in the neighborhood.

If the church has anyone who can do sculpture, creative efforts expressing peace motifs could be prominently displayed. Crafts can also be used. Roy Johnsen, pastor of the Central Baptist Church in Williamsport, Pennsylvania, has produced woodcrafts that often speak to the peace of Christ. Many of the proceeds of his sales were donated to the Baptist Peace Fellowship. His Communion sets and dove necklaces have been used as peacemaking exchange gifts with Baptists in the Soviet Union, Nicaragua, and the Middle East.

The Verbal Arts

While good preaching is surely an art form, a poet can often say in a few words what a mediocre preacher fails to say in an hour-long sermon. Poetry can deliver God's Word as surely as a sermon can, so our poets as well as our preachers need to be heard.

Poets such as b. f. maiz, a campus chaplain in Cleveland, can be invited to do readings or recitations at special events. If someone in the congregation writes poetry, he or she should be given a place in the service to read a poem or have it published in the church newsletter. Perhaps poems can be presented on a poster, using the skills in the visual arts of some other congregant. Even if there are no writers of poetry in the congregation, appropriate poems could still be read as part of the worship experience.

Children often enjoy writing poetry, especially if given a particular theme and structure. One common form is the cinquain poem. Line one is a one-word noun, such as "peace," "friend," "war," and so on. Line two is two adjectives that describe the noun. Line three is three gerunds ("-ing" words) that describe the noun. Line four is four words that express a feeling about the noun. Line five concludes the poem with a one-word synonym. The children's poems can be displayed in the church or read as part of the worship service.

Storytelling is an ancient art experiencing revival in this country. Much of the Bible consists of stories that were passed down orally before being put into writing. Paul Dekar, a Canadian Baptist historian, has brought to life many stories of Baptist peacemakers whose journeys of faith and ministry can inform our own. He has told these stories at many Baptist Peace Fellowship conferences around the world. Some have recently been published in his book *For the Healing of the Nations: Baptist Peacemakers*.[3] Telling stories of our historical heritage helps weave the generations together. If the younger generation doesn't learn its history in a compelling way, then it is impoverished.

Some sermons can be turned into stories. All Saints Day (formally November 1, but could be observed on the first Sunday in November) is a good time to tell the story of a peacemaking Christian—that person's context, the issues faced, and how she or he was faithful to Christ's call during that particular time in history. Children's sermons can provide an opportunity for instruction for the children through story, and if the story has depth and integrity, it will also speak to the adults who are listening. Storytelling through the use of folktales or the reading of children's books on peace themes can also be effective.

Movement Arts

Dance is an art form some of our forebears might be disturbed to know is used in churches today. But dance was an expression of Hebrew worship, from David, who danced before the ark, to the psalmist who proclaimed "Praise God with timbrel and dance!" (see 2 Samuel 6:14 and Psalm 150:4). Skilled liturgical dancers can interpret through movement peace Scriptures, songs, or poems. Simple dance motions can also be taught to the congregation as a whole; hand motions or the use of American sign language with songs can be taught for variation or if dancing is too uncomfortable for some.

Dance has played a major role in the freedom movement in South Africa. Where people suffer, dancing can become an expression of hope. When hopes are fulfilled in victory, dance becomes the exuberance of joy. If a congregation has journeyed together in a peace initiative, there may come moments when spontaneous dancing is a natural expression of the congregation's feelings. Such jubilant outbursts have happened at various conferences, but most

---

[3]Paul R. Dekar, *For the Healing of the Nations: Baptist Peacemakers* (Macon, Ga.: Smyth & Helwys Publishing, 1993).

local churches are still too restrained!

Drama can be an effective way of communicating peace messages as well as using the talents of a number of church members. Many plays and skits on peace themes are available.[4] Writers in the church should be encouraged to come up with their own skits, perhaps expressing a particular theme in an upcoming worship service or relating to a peace project the church has undertaken. Puppets are another way drama can be presented, involving not just the puppeteers but also those skilled in making the puppets.

Arts Festivals

An arts festival can bring together a variety of artistic expressions around one theme. Organizing a festival takes a lot of work and coordination, but the event can be a major one for the life of the congregation and even the larger community. The First Baptist Church of Lafayette, Indiana, played a leading role in organizing a religious arts festival for its city on the theme "Artisans of Peace, Weavers of Life." Many of the area churches were involved in hosting portions of the festival. The festival included paintings, slides, calligraphy, choirs, drama, handbells, and workshops in various arts and crafts. There was even an exhibit on liturgical vestments and the language of clerical robes. An exhibition of works by over thirty artists was set up at First Baptist Church during one of the festival weeks.

> *I had a dream of having a peace fair in a parking lot of First Baptist Church of Lafayette, Indiana. I was trying to build consensus among several clergy and lay leaders in the community, but one person effectively blocked the direction I was going. A member of the Religious Arts Festival was open to the idea of their hosting a Peace Day on the theme "Seek Peace and Pursue It." The St. Thomas Aquinas Center was willing to host the day at the center. We had activities for children, youth, and adults, closing with a worship celebration. The following*

---

[4]See the listing in *Peacemaking Creatively Through the Arts* by Phyllis Vos Wezeman (Educational Ministries, Inc., 2861-C Saturn St., Brea, CA 92621, 1990), 229. A number of plays are contained in Ingrid Roger's *Swords into Plowshares: A Collection of Plays about Peace and Social Justice* (Elgin, Ill.: Brethren Press, 1983).

*year our theme was "Artisans of Peace, Weavers of Life."
Someone's no was not closure but a new direction (though
I did not feel that way at first). By tying Peace Day to the
Religious Arts Festival, I saw new ways of communicating,
learning, teaching, and experiencing peacemaking. Through
the arts, biblical peacemaking was able to transcend, trans-
form, and translate biblical peacemaking into realities that
broadened the current modalities of peacemaking. The creativity of the participants of all ages brought forth new ways of
relating to one another and the creation. The arts related at
different levels that touched people in unexpected ways. What
was also exciting for me was to see social activists in our area
not snubbing the arts as a superfluous exercise; they participated. We will never know the full impact of Peace Day. But
this I do know: "So shall my word be that goeth forth out of my
mouth: it shall not return unto me void, but it shall accomplish
that which I please, and it shall prosper in the thing whereto I
sent it" (Isaiah 55:11, KJV).*

—Ernie Elder, Lafayette, Indiana

There are more ways to use the arts in the service of peacemaking
than anyone can imagine, for the imagination God has put within
us is infinitely creative. Turn that creativity loose in your church,
not only for peacemaking but for all expressions of Christian life
and community.

Chapter 7

Affinity Groups

Small groups are to peace movements and to church renewal movements what cells are to living organisms. The small peace-making group within a local church can be the most basic, intensive, and vital expression of peacemaking ministry while also serving as a building block for the larger-scale mobilizing of people to bring about change in a society.

A small group can take heartfelt concerns and lofty ideals and translate them into specific actions. By joining together we create an accountability that pushes us past merely talking about issues into doing something productive. Moving stories on the news or from the pulpit can stir our hearts, and a conflict at the crisis point can deeply disturb us. However, unless we organize ourselves, the good intentions generated by these proddings of our conscience will evaporate, leaving nothing of substance. By organizing a group to share, study, and act together, the good intentions can be fleshed out.

The author of Ecclesiastes speaks of the value of having other people as partners in our journeys:

Two are better than one, because they have a good reward for their toil. For if they fall, one will lift up the other; but woe to one who is alone and falls and does not have another to help. Again, if two lie together, they keep warm; but how can one keep warm alone? And though one might prevail against another, two will withstand one. A threefold cord is not quickly broken (Ecclesiastes 4:9-12).

The journey of peacemaking can lead to confronting difficult issues within oneself: feelings of violent anger, the loss of long-held values or myths, and so on. One may even be brought to points of action that require a courage seldom exercised before. Having friends to share that journey, to provide a listening ear and offer the support of companionship, can make the difference between moving ahead with courageous purpose or slipping into wistful irrelevancy as the world goes through its turmoil.

Many local congregations have formed peace groups, some for long periods of time, others for shorter-range projects. The Dorchester Temple Baptist Church in Boston formed a peacemakers' group around the nuclear freeze campaign in the early eighties, which was then reconstituted to act around Central American issues in the mid-eighties.

Other congregations have peace groups that sustain their life for years, covering a multitude of issues. For many concerned individuals, however, their church is not very supportive of their involvement in peace concerns. For such people, the support group might be a community group or a regional peace fellowship. There is much to be gained, though, if the journey of those who have made a major commitment in peacemaking can be woven into the corporate life of the congregation. Instead of living a schizophrenic life of spirituality and worship on the one hand and politics and action on the other, these two worlds can be integrated. Faith can have a holistic expression in worship and action in the world.

The presence of a peacemaking group will also give fuller expression to the whole congregation of the scope of ministry that flows out of the people of God. The group will make the body of Christ more whole by using the gifts of the group's members and providing a channel for their ministry to be carried out. The group also can provide a prophetic witness within the congregation to stretch all members to deeper discipleship within the contemporary world.

Getting Started

Every new project requires someone willing to put in the effort to get the ball rolling. Often organizational and personal inertia needs to be overcome, and one or two people willing to invest the time and energy to start a group are needed. They must have at least two qualifications: a vision for the group clear enough and relevant enough to draw people, and a willingness to do the basic, mundane work of getting organized. The Baptist Peace Fellowship of North America has a booklet, "Recipe for Peacemaking: Which Ingredient Can You Supply," which provides material on both a vision for the group and practical ideas for involving congregation members in peacework.[1]

Laypeople generally make the best leaders of a small group, though a pastor may help stimulate and state the guiding vision. A layperson can often provide more focused energy and not get swamped by the broad range of congregational and institutional responsibilities that can weigh on the pastor. Lay leadership also provides some grassroots ownership of the ministry of the group, which can help minimize conflict or resistance in the congregation about having a peace group. Unless the pastoral leadership is strong or the church's peacemaking commitment clearly established, having the pastor as the main promoter and organizer of a peace group can deepen an adversarial relationship between pastor and people. If the pastor does not attend, the group leaders should keep him or her informed of the group's activities on a regular basis.

The vision of the group can be formed around a specific issue: mobilizing to act about a war, community violence, racism, conversion of local military industries, and so on. Or the group can be formed around a spiritual growth concern such as studying what the Bible says about peace or justice. The group may have an initial focus to relate to a mission project in a conflict zone, such as Haiti or Nicaragua or Eastern Europe, perhaps looking into church partnerships or mission work trips as the initial organizing activity. The Dorchester Temple Baptist Church peacemaking group was revived when a member of the congregation visited Nicaragua with a group of school teachers.

In the summer of 1984 I spent ten days traveling in Nicaragua with a group of North American teachers, hosted by representatives of the Nicaraguan educators' union. I went eagerly, praying for a clear perspective on the four-year-old Sandinista revolution and on the U.S.-supported "contra war"

---

[1]See Appendix B for BPFNA address.

*that the Reagan administration had been escalating to under-
mine the new government. My exposure there to the civilian,
and often Christian, casualties of the war, gained through
meeting with American Baptist missionaries as well as with
teachers, was deeply disturbing. Struck by the spiritual blind-
ness of U.S. policy, I returned with a profound sense of responsibility to share what I had seen and heard.*

*Upon my return, friends of mine within my church who had
been involved in a peacemakers group encouraged me to give
a slide presentation about the trip for interested members of
the congregation. That evening of sharing turned out to be a
catalyst for a new season in the peacemakers group experience.
New folks joined, and we continued to meet weekly to pray, to
learn about Central American history, to build ties with Nicaraguan Christians, and to engage in peaceful actions of protest
against our government's policies. It was wonderful to see the
trip spawn such a wholehearted response and to find the yoke
and burden of my personal sense of responsibility made light,
and even joyful, through our fellowship and work together.*
                    —Scott Walker, Boston, Massachusetts

The group's initial vision should not be so detailed that other
people cannot help shape the direction of the group. A question
rather than an answer can be the best starting point. Then one of the
first tasks of the newly formed group will be to shape a shared set
of goals so that the vision is more broadly owned.

The next step is to invite others to participate. Announcements
of a meeting can be made through the church bulletin and newspaper or at the worship service. Identify people in the congregation
you know who might be interested in the issue. Approach them
directly at church or over the telephone. There is no substitute for
direct, one-on-one invitations. The organizers need to talk to people
personally and take the time to listen to other people's concerns as
well as sharing the organizing vision. Often those conversations
help provide a sharper focus and a more broadly shared vision for
the group. A simple information sheet can be prepared that sketches
out the vision and provides the names and phone numbers of the
contact people. Once the group is going, make further invitations
through information tables in the back of the church or at coffee
hour or through hosting an educational forum on the issue.

The initial invitations should be made with a tentative date in mind that can be firmed up in discussion with those who indicate an interest in participating. A home or small church meeting room, perhaps a parlor, would be the best location. Plan the agenda carefully, being sure that the meeting will not drag on too long. Begin with a brief devotional related to the theme of the meeting. If people don't know each other well, take some time for introductions. Invite participants to tell what stimulated their interest in peace issues, particularly in the topic at hand.

Once the group is introduced to one another, don't try to solve all the world's problems in an initial meeting! Rather, present the proposed project or give a brief educational presentation on the issue. Allow plenty of time for discussion and interaction. If a particular project is being suggested, present the necessary steps for its implementation, including an outline of costs and tasks. The agenda should include a discussion about the next step, whether or not to hold another meeting or form an ongoing group, and who will make commitments to the new group or particular tasks. The group might want to set a specific point at which to end the project or at least reevaluate commitments and direction. Set a specific time and place for the next meeting while everyone is together. Close with a time of prayer about the issue and your commitments to act on it.

Those involved in leading the group or hoping to start one might benefit from reading a book about peacemaking groups. Glen Stassen's *Journey into Peacemaking*[2] is an excellent guide for new peacemaking groups. It contains thirteen sessions of study, prayer, and action suggestions that can help a group get grounded biblically and relationally as they seek to act constructively in the world. *Peace and Justice Ministry: A Practical Guide* by Richard Taylor[3] is a basic guidebook for how to organize and run a peace-and-justice group within a congregation. It contains helpful lists of things to do, from constructing an agenda and group decision making to outreach and evaluation.

---

[2] Glen Stassen, *Journey into Peacemaking* (Memphis: Brotherhood Commission, Southern Baptist Convention, 1983).

[3] Richard K. Taylor, *Peace and Justice Ministry: A Practical Guide* (Dubuque, Iowa: Brown-Roa, 1994).

Group Life

A peacemaking group is more than a committee; it can become a community. People in the group will journey together in ways that may be life transforming, often bringing them into experiences that stretch their faith, realign their values, and shake their world-views. They will come into close contact with profoundly disturbing problems and struggle to discover God's call and provision in a very complex context. They may experience deep sorrows and ecstatic joy together. Peacemaking involves life-and-death issues at times, so a serious commitment will bring the group members into a world that is both emotionally intense and intellectually stimulating.

Some congregational peace groups will meet monthly or bi-weekly, while others will choose to meet on a weekly basis. Yet others will gather only for special events, with a few people acting as a steering committee that plans the group's projects and programs. The peace group in the North Hills Community Baptist Church in Pittsburgh meets weekly. They study, pray, and develop projects. They sponsor the church's annual observance of Peace Sunday and lead the service. They have sent a member to work in a refugee camp in Croatia. They also have worked in partnership with other groups, such as the local Habitat for Humanity project and a health ministry to low-income people. They have traveled to Washington, D.C., to demonstrate for handgun control and have participated in a "gang summit" in their own city. Their actions emerge out of their steady core of meeting, study, and prayer.

As we engage in the peacemaking journey together, shared spiritual disciplines can deepen the bonds among the group members and between the group and the sustaining grace of God. Shared spiritual disciplines (see chapter 8) are especially needed if the group is engaged in a longer-term project or one with some risk involved, such as traveling to a war zone or committing civil disobedience. Bible study, prayer, discussion, and reflection can help members keep a Christ-centered focus and root their hope deeper than any ebb and flow of historical events.

A wealth of biblical material on peacemaking is available, although much of it may be unfamiliar to most church members. Bible studies can be held periodically as ways to ground the group's actions in a more thoughtful faith basis.[4] Journaling can be another way to process one's views and experiences. If members of the group take time to share their insights from journaling or from reflections on readings about peacemaking, they will grow in both wisdom and commitment.[5] Group prayer can become more than a perfunctory opening and closing of a meeting. Together the group members can process their own feelings and concerns before God. One peace group found themselves spending a third of their meeting time in prayer, confronting their own anger toward the government and their own fears about taking action.

Decisions in the group are best handled by consensus, which forces the group to practice peacemaking among themselves. Consensus decision making values the contribution of each person to the process and the fact that each has something at stake in the decision. It also gives broader ownership of the decisions made by the group, which heightens the commitment to follow through on those decisions.

To decide by consensus the group first discusses the proposals. When a decision point is reached, ask if there is consensus. Solicit especially the input of those who have been silent. Ask if anyone has a problem with the proposal. If there are problems, ask people to state their concerns and see if the proposal can be acceptably adapted to address those concerns. The result can often be a stronger proposal. If the proposal cannot be adapted to address the concerns of those who cannot agree with it, then ask whether they feel strong enough about the issue to block the consensus or whether they will

---

[4]My *Bible Study Guide: War and Peace* is a comprehensive workbook on biblical teachings on war and peace. It provides biblical texts, introductory notes, questions, and space to write answers and reflections. The study guide is available in Spanish as well as English from National Ministries Literature Resources, P.O. Box 851, Valley Forge, PA 19482. The Presbyterian Peacemaking Program (100 Witherspoon St., Louisville, KY 40202-1396) has an excellent series of Bible studies on peacemaking in Luke, Isaiah, Corinthians, Jeremiah, Acts, the Psalms, as well as on topics such as violence, conflict resolution, and the family. The Kerygma Program has a study, *Shalom: A Study of the Biblical Concept of Peace*, available from 300 Mt. Lebanon Blvd., Suite 205, Pittsburgh, PA 15234.

[5]*A Peacemaker's Journal* can be a tool for group reflection and journaling. It contains fifty-two quotes on peace themes, particularly on the inner journey of the peacemaker, with room to write or draw. *A Peacemaker's Journal* is available from National Ministries Literature Resources (see address in footnote 4).

accede to the position taken by the others in the group. For genuine consensus it is vital that those who block consensus be valued and not bullied into agreement. There are plenty of times when the lone minority voice was proved right in the long run. The wisdom of dissenters must be respected, especially in groups that claim to dissent against the injustices and domination of other groups and social systems.

Justice also needs to be practiced within the group. Lessons in the struggles against sexism and racism have revealed some of the subtle and not-so-subtle ways that domination can be carried out, even by people with good intentions. Talking too much, taking charge before others can volunteer, condescending, restating what another person has said clearly, intellectualizing when it's appropriate to share personal feelings, and solving problems before others have a chance to contribute—all these are tools of control that will undermine the efforts of committed peacemakers. If such problems plague a group, honestly confronting the problems with others or within oneself is the necessary step to create more equitable relationships. There may be times of painful dialogue, but faithfully persevering in the process of honesty will pay off with deepened trust and respect for one another.

The life of a peacemaking group may fall into a natural rhythm. Periods of activity around campaigns, congressional votes, trips, and demonstrations are offset by quieter times when no issues are pushing to the forefront and participants are able to catch their breath. The rhythms of events and group life can be a dynamic within which the group works. See the quiet times as opportunities to deepen the group spiritually by doing Bible study or participating in shared spiritual disciplines. Slow times are good to engage in background study, perhaps picking a book that the whole group can read and discuss. Relationship-building activities can just be fun get-togethers. If the group has engaged in difficult activities together, such as a civil disobedience action or a trip to another country, more relaxed settings of a cookout or picnic can allow for a different kind of bonding to take place.

Part of a group life cycle is death. There comes a time for all groups to die. It is healthy to acknowledge when a particular group needs to disband. The warning symptoms may be a more muddled focus, lagging attendance at group events, and a lessened energy level in the group. Rather than just letting the group wither away, the group can be ended explicitly and with celebration, leaving those involved with a more positive feeling. Have a closing party at which you can share stories and pictures, express thanks to individuals, and recall victories and defeats. Close with prayers of thanksgiving for the journey you have had together and intercession for the needs that still exist.

Sometimes, as the issues shift—from the nuclear freeze to Central America, from the Middle East to Korea, from South Africa to neighborhood violence—the makeup and commitments of the group will shift as well. Letting one group die and another be born to focus on a new concern can help with the transitions. It allows people to make clean decisions about whether to continue, and such breaks permit new people to join at the beginning stages and help shape the nature of the group. Some groups will have a broad peacemaking vision, in which case disbanding and reconstituting around a new issue may be unnecessary. But if not, few things are more deadly to a group than losing focus and limping around looking for a new concern around which to center. Clear vision, clear times to end the project, and new beginnings can keep the church's interest in and commitment to peace strong.

> The Salvador Partners Mission Group of Central Baptist Church in Wayne, Pennsylvania, began ten years ago as the Sanctuary Task Force. At that time a nucleus of a half-dozen leaders first coordinated congregational study and approval of becoming a "sanctuary church" for Central American refugees. When we received a Salvadoran man seeking sanctuary, the task force arranged hospitality and speaking engagements for him. As the realities and needs in El Salvador changed, so did the focus of Salvador Partners—from working with public sanctuary to working with partners in El Salvador. The Salvador Partners Mission Group, though small, continues to flourish with the full support of the congregation. We have kept our focus on El Salvador, and although other mission groups deal with other issues, we have tried to find common threads in our work for peace and justice. We have evolved as the situation changed and sought to keep ourselves and our congregation educated about the politics, the economics, and the theology

emerging in El Salvador.

Perhaps most importantly, we have made our partnerships real through personal contact. We have touched each others' lives and challenged each others' views so that we can truly grow together as partners. The people in our partner communities are not just names; they are real people with stories to tell, arms to hug us, and tears of joy and pain to share.
—Ellen Green, Trappe, Pennsylvania

Connections

Maintaining connections to those outside the group is important for the work of the group in the church and its involvement with the larger community. Good connections should be maintained with the larger body of the congregation. Identifying the leadership team of the group helps people in the church know whom to contact about events or to join the group. A spokesperson should be identified to be sure that announcements are made in the bulletin, church services, and newsletters in an appropriate and timely fashion. If the group is more than an ad hoc cluster to examine a particular issue, it might be worth exploring some form of structured representation on a church board or council. This would give the peacemaking group an official place within the church structure as well as a formalized channel into the decision-making processes of the church. Some churches have a social concerns, social action, or missions committee that may be the appropriate body to which a peacemakers' group could relate.

The group may also decide to be a part of a larger issue network in the area or even to participate in a number of networks. Many metropolitan areas have Central American networks. A group focused on Central America would want to be linked into the area network to keep in touch with upcoming events and actions. Members of the group might want to participate in tours sponsored by the regional network. Identify a person in the group to be the liaison to the network. This lets the network know whom to contact when they need to get the word out quickly regarding a special concern or action. The contact person may also want to attend the meetings of the network planning group. It takes quite a bit of time to be a contact person because you are effectively involved in two groups, but these linkages provide the glue that holds a movement together. An effective connection to an action network can multiply the impact of your group's work as well as provide the inspiration and stimulation of being part of a larger movement for social or political change.

Chapter 8

Nurturing the Inward Journey of Peacemakers

The Teacher in Ecclesiastes said, "Wisdom is better than weapons of war" (9:18). Such wisdom comes only through deliberate discipline and reflection. James 3:17 describes it as "the wisdom from above," a product of an intimate walk with God. The peacemaking journey is long and fraught with many dangers, defeats, and dilemmas. To sustain oneself and one's companions along the way, the inward spiritual journey needs to be intentionally nurtured.

The front lines of peacemaking often lie within our own hearts. That is where hatreds fester, fears lurk, and greed devours our souls. The inner self is also where perseverance is born, where hope is generated, and where courage takes root. In Jesus' parable of the sower, he spoke of the seed that fell in the rocky soil. It sprang up quickly but then withered in the heat of the sun, for it had no root (Mark 4:5-6). Though Jesus was referring to the response of people to the gospel message, the parable also is apt for the short-term efforts of many peacemakers. As they encounter the scorching difficulties of intractable and even violent conflicts, early enthusiasm and idealism can fade away. Paths of cynicism or self-serving can be taken, instead of paying the price to pursue a vision of peace. Roots need to be put down. We need nourishment from deep sources within us that tap into the wellsprings of God's Spirit.

Spiritual Disciplines

The traditional spiritual disciplines of prayer, meditation, Bible study, and fasting all can nourish the peacemaker. Prayer is the vital communication link between us and God. Quality communication makes any relationship, and in the divine-human interaction, a life of prayer becomes a dynamo for action in the world. In prayer we can offer our own troubles and the troubles of the world that burden us to the One who said to the wind and waves, "Peace! Be still!" (Mark 4:39). We recognize God's sovereignty over all the baffling events of history's flow through our lives, and God hears our cries of anguish for those who suffer. God also touches us in the mystery of prayer so that "the peace of God, which surpasses all understanding" (Philippians 4:7) will hold our minds and hearts secure even when the rational mind is battered by the evidence of human brutality and folly.

Bible study can be specifically geared to peace. The student of the Bible can do a topical study of war and peace. Workbooks such as my *Bible Study Guide on War and Peace* and *A Bible Study Guide on Conflict Resolution*[1] can give a disciplined structure to one's biblical investigations. The Presbyterian Peacemaking Program publishes an annual "Biblical Witness to Peacemaking" that gives daily readings from the Bible on a wide range of peace themes for the entire year.[2] Such aids can be used in one's daily devotions. Read a passage, study it, reflect on it, and listen to what God might say through it about the situations you face.

Meditation is quieting ourselves so we can reflect on a particular point of growth or need. It can be intentional, focused thinking. It can be prayer in which one's inner being is quietly and openly directed toward God. It can be mental silence so that deep voices within ourselves can emerge. Sometimes it is helpful to give content or an initial jumping-off point to our meditations through the use of Bible passages or the writings of people who have expressed their own journey of peacemaking.[3]

---

[1] See resource listing for information on how to obtain these study guides.

[2] To obtain a copy of "The Biblical Witness to Peacemaking," contact the Presbyterian Peacemaking Program, 100 Witherspoon St., Louisville, KY 40202-1396 (502-569-5784).

[3] My book *A Peacemaker's Journal* is one aid to meditation. It is a collection of quotes on peacemaking themes with room for writing reflections and poetry or drawing.

Fasting is an alien practice to many North American Christians, but it has a long history in our faith as well as in the faiths of many other religious folk. Fasting is a disciplining of one's desires, expressed most graphically by refraining from eating. Radical fasts involve not eating at all. More modest fasts might involve skipping a meal or drinking juices. Fasting is best done in conjunction with prayer so that the inner issues become the focal point rather than the mere missing of food. The point of fasting is not deprivation. Rather, one's desires are focused on a transcendent need for self or for others. Since wars are rooted in corrupted desires (see James 4:1-10), fasting seeks to develop mastery over our desires. Fasting is usually a private matter, though at times fasting can be a group discipline with a witness to the larger community. Prior to and during the Gulf War, the Baptist Peace Fellowship of North America called for people to commit themselves to daily prayer and weekly fasting for peace. Over fifteen hundred Baptist women and men joined in that commitment.

The struggle to control appetites, whether literally (in the case of food) or metaphorically (in other acquisitive habits), is clearly a pertinent issue for all of us who live in the so-called first world. The very fact that, in an age when sixty thousand die daily from starvation and nutrition-related diseases, our media is crowded with advertising for diet plans is proof enough that something is seriously out of balance.

On a larger, public scale, the issue of uncontrolled appetites is identified by James as the root of war. "What causes wars?" he asks. "Is it not your passions"—your cravings, your appetites—"which are at war within you? You desire and do not have; so you kill. And you covet and cannot obtain; so you fight and wage war" (4:1-2, paraphrased).

Seen in this light, the cravings of individuals and the cravings of nation-states—though obviously different in scale—are parallel afflictions. To fast, therefore, encourages us to acknowledge our own personal temptation and inclination to gluttony and gives us a manageable, remedial step toward health. It also helps us identify with the gluttony in which we participate on a much larger scale.

Bringing our personal habits under control, adjusting them so that they nudge us toward health rather than heart attack,

toward life rather than death—these are among the reasons for
fasting. And as we do this, we become aware of the need to bring
public, corporate habits (policies) under control; we face the
need for policies that nudge our nations toward health and life.
                              —Ken Sehested, Memphis, Tennessee

Nurturing One Another

Within the congregation are ways we can nurture one another in
our inward journeys as peacemakers. Pastors, teachers, and group
leaders can explicitly encourage and teach the spiritual disciplines,
emphasizing that activists need to nurture their inner selves as do
people who take to quietness more naturally. Activists can be so
busy doing peace work that they can crash into despair or burnout
without realizing they were in danger, so a word of encouragement
to foster a deep peace within is a word well spoken.

A peacemaking group within a congregation can adopt a group
discipline as a part of their regular experience. Our peacemakers
group at the Dorchester Temple Baptist Church in Boston would
begin their meetings with a member leading in a brief Bible study
or reflection on a reading. Then we would pray. Besides interces-
sory prayers for people in war zones, we spent much time processing our own feelings of anger toward U.S. officials. It can be easy
for some peacemakers to love those far-off labeled as "enemy" by
our government, and then in self-righteousness hate the "enemy"
close to home, the "enemy" whose policies we oppose. Through
group prayer such feelings can be processed and purified. Then the
actions planned in the rest of the meeting flow from clearer minds
and hearts.

Often a peacemaking group experiences a rhythm of intense
action followed by quiet. As demonstrations or lobbying campaigns
are underway, the activity takes all the group's energy and focus.
But during the "down times," there can be a nurturing of the inner
person, a process shared and supported by the group. More intense
times of Bible study and spiritual formation can be held when the
agenda is less crowded with the pressure of the urgent. Those times
are normal and even necessary for group life, so that when the action
heats up again there will be deeper roots from which to draw
sustenance.

Loving Our Enemies

The greatest spiritual discipline for peacemakers is loving our enemies. This discipline was explicitly and plainly given to us by Jesus: "You have heard that it was said, 'You shall love your neighbor and hate your enemy.' But I say to you, Love your enemies and pray for those who persecute you" (Matthew 5:43-44). Loving our enemies has many different meanings. Our first question might be, "Who is my enemy?" During the Cold War the enemy of the United States was said to be the Soviet Union, along with smaller enemies, such as the Nicaraguan Sandinistas, Cubans, Vietnamese, and other Communists. Now the national enemies list contains some old hangovers from the Cold War era, such as Cuba and North Korea, and new villains, including Muslim fundamentalists and Iraq. Many U.S. citizens would agree with the government assessment of these opponents as enemies and accept distorted stereotypes as truth. Feelings of hatred can be stirred up at times even with little understanding of who the "enemy" really is. Peacemakers, on the other hand, would tend to learn more about the opposed country, often through direct contact. They thus frequently have a different perspective. While not always agreeing with or accepting the policies of "enemy" countries, they develop ties of love and respect to people which counter the hatred around them. Loving our national enemies has often been a part of the peacemaking journey.

Loving the "enemies" at home has been harder for peacemakers. The people in our government who shape policies with which we disagree and people in our own congregations who go along and cheer those policies are the "enemy" in our hearts and minds, though perhaps never acknowledged as such. While Communists and Islamic fundamentalists don't produce an immediate response of anger, conservative politicians, military personnel, and fundamentalist Christians engaged in conservative politics can make a peacemaker's blood boil. One noted Christian peace figure once wrote about Henry Kissinger as a demonic person, having passed from humanity into evil incarnate. That is as dehumanizing as calling the Soviet Union the "Evil Empire." On the other hand, certain forces, institutions, and historical dynamics are clearly destructive to human existence and well-being. Walter

Wink's three-volume work on "the powers" provides a stimulating, biblically based look at such forces and ways that Christians can engage them for peace and justice.[4] How then does the Christian peacemaker separate the persons involved in evil systems and institutions from those "powers"? Do we love just the person who is the "enemy," or also the force or institution?

Honesty requires peacemakers to identify their true enemies. How do we distort what the other side or person is saying or values? How do we fear them and act out of the projections born of those fears? Jesus spoke about not pointing out the speck in the other person's eye until we have dealt with the beam in our own (Matthew 7:1-5). Peacemakers need to apply the same perspectives toward our theological and political enemies for the sake of our own spiritual health. Some activists labor sacrificially for peace and justice at a global level but have wretched conflicts in their own intimate relationships, sometimes due to their unjust treatment of those closest to them. Even worse is the enmity within our own selves. Augustine said, "Imagine the vanity of thinking that your enemy can do you more damage than your enmity." We can be "politically correct" and yet spiritually bankrupt, saving the world but losing our own souls.

Sam Keen has produced a classic study of the psychology of enmity in his book *Faces of the Enemy: Reflections of the Hostile Imagination*.[5] Using political art and cartoons, Keen shows how enemy thinking is developed and manipulated to the point where people dehumanize one another so they can then kill. He argues that we must struggle against the entire war system, including the institutions that shape people's thinking about war and the psychological defense mechanisms we employ. Peacemakers can get a good handle on the institutions but miss our own inner enmities. Keen encourages us to "listen to what the enemy says about you, and you will learn the truth you have repressed. To

---

[4] Walter Wink, *Naming the Powers: The Language of Power in the New Testament* (Minneapolis: Augsburg/Fortress, 1984); *Unmasking the Powers: The Invisible Forces That Determine Human Existence* (Minneapolis: Augsburg/Fortress, 1993); *Engaging the Powers: Discernment and Resistance in a World of Domination* (Minneapolis: Augsburg/Fortress, 1992).

[5] Sam Keen, *Faces of the Enemy: Reflections of the Hostile Imagination* (San Francisco: Harper & Row, 1986).

come to greater self-understanding, borrow the eyes of the alien, see yourself from afar."[6]

To learn how to love our enemies, a support group within the church, perhaps the peacemakers group, can be a place where we can be honest in identifying those who spark our rage and hatred. Name them. Then begin to pray for them by name. Pray that God will bless them and help them grow. Pray for your own feelings, too—for the cynicism, bitterness, fear, and envy of success that distorts how you perceive both yourself and the other. Loving your enemy doesn't mean you will agree, give in, or cease to struggle for justice and peace. It does mean that you will keep humanizing your enemies in your own mind, thus humanizing yourself. It is a work of God to replace the dynamics of hate with the dynamics of love, and confession and prayer are the footsteps of the journey.

---

[6] Ibid., 95.

Chapter 9

Church Partnerships

Church partnerships across national, racial/ethnic, cultural, class, or language divides can be a special project of congregational peacemaking. Partnerships with other congregations, sometimes called "sister churches," have been established to demonstrate Christ's reconciling work in contexts where political or social conflicts have split people apart. Sometimes the partnerships are with congregations in the same city. Other partnerships span thousands of miles as churches are linked across "enemy" borders. Church partnerships generate both excitement and frustration. By looking carefully at what is involved and setting realistic and mutually acceptable goals, a church partnership can become a moving, learning experience that bonds people together in profound ways.

Why Establish Partner Congregations?

The divisions among humanity caused by racism, international conflicts, class differences, language, fear, and ignorance are elements of the context into which the gospel comes. The biblical message is that Christ has become the unifying bond reaching across the barriers. As Ephesians 2:13-16 puts it:

But now in Christ Jesus you who once were far off have been brought near by the blood of Christ. For he is our peace; in his flesh he has made both groups into one and has broken down the dividing wall, that is, the hostility between us . . . that he might create in himself one new humanity in place of the two, thus making peace, and might reconcile both groups to God in one body through the cross, thus putting to death that hostility through it.

Central to our theology is the unity of the body of Christ, God's people.

However, central to our church experience is segregation according to the world's divisions. The old saying that Sunday at 11:00 A.M. is the most segregated hour still holds true. We can find some acceptable reasons for that segregation (people prefer to worship in their own cultural forms, for example), but the main reason is the history of Christian accommodation to the sins of society, a history we still live out in the present. Establishing partner congregations is one way to try to move beyond the history of division and break out of the confines of segregation. It is one way to resist the creation of new barriers erected by conflict and to participate in the building of bridges of understanding and solidarity.

Few churches are genuinely multicultural. Churches are geographically defined, if not to a particular neighborhood parish, certainly to a town, metropolitan area, and nation. Most congregations are made up predominately of members from one ethnic group and reflect that group's culture, even though there may be a sprinkling of members from other ethnic groups or cultures. So for there to be a vital expression of Christian unity, intentional efforts need to be undertaken to connect to congregations representing different parts of the human and Christian family. Partner churches can give concrete expression to the work of reconciliation that the Bible sees as central.

The sister-church relationship is a life-giving experience. It has changed lives. Our congregation has grown in faith and understanding as well as the individuals who have participated in our delegations. Our young people tell us that they will not be the same. They won't. I see it in the development of their faith.
—Charles Syverson, Palo Alto, California

How to Start an International Partnership

A congregational partnership is first and foremost a relationship. As a relationship, its genesis is more likely to take place through face-to-face encounters than in some semi-arbitrary pairing. Formalized efforts to match congregations have a poor track record and tend to collapse quickly. They are the dating-service version of congregational pairing. So it is not recommended to contact a denominational or ecumenical office to seek a partner church. However, if the church feels it has no other options and wants to pursue a pairing, it can check with the denominational mission office for a recommendation. The process may take a while and demand perseverance and creativity, so those engaged in initiating the partnership project need to be prepared for a long, slow process. Some churches in fact *have* successfully established church partnerships by going through denominational channels.

We have an official sister-church relationship with Primera Iglesia Bautista in Corinto, Nicaragua. We have had an active relationship since July 1985. In February 1984 we were challenged by Gustavo Parajón and Steven Heneise, both American Baptist missionaries in Nicaragua, to form a sister-church relationship if we were seriously interested in knowing Nicaragua's people and understanding their social, political, and religious realities. With the help of Tomás Téllez, executive secretary of the Nicaraguan Baptist Convention, we were initially paired with the church in Leon, but due to pastoral difficulties, we were paired with Corinto.

We have maintained our relationship with monthly phone calls, weekly prayers for one another, letters, special recommitment worship services, support by First Baptist Church for specific projects at Primera Iglesia Bautista, and through delegations visiting Corinto. These face-to-face visits have been powerful experiences that have done the most to solidify and strengthen the relationship.

—Charles Syverson, Palo Alto, California

The best way to find an international partner church is for someone to travel. When people are on a friendship tour or a mission work tour, they have the opportunity to see other churches and meet the sisters and brothers in those congregations. The bond is created face-to-face rather than dossier-to-dossier, resulting in heart-to-heart connections. When Grace Morgan of Wauwatosa, Wisconsin, visited the Baptist Church on the Marzahner Promenade in East Berlin in the old German Democratic Republic, her personal tie initiated the relationship that grew between that church and her home congregation, Underwood Baptist. When John Detwyler served as a volunteer missionary in Nicaragua, he visited the rural area of Los Gutiérrez Norte, where he met the pastor of the Getsemaní Baptist Church. Their relationship grew, and when John returned to his home congregation of Emmanuel Baptist in Schenectady, New York, he suggested the churches link up.

If a church member is going on such a trip, preparations should be made in advance to consider whether the church wants to pair up with another congregation. The pastor and the church's leadership body should discuss the idea, and if it is viewed favorably, a committee could be drawn up or the proposal passed on to the appropriate standing board or committee. Then preparations can be made to send some items from the church with the traveler, such as a photo of church members, a church bulletin, and a small, symbolic gift. Many partner-church relations begin only after the initial contact is made and the traveler returns full of enthusiasm about the people met in the other country.

The formal discussion about a partnership can be initiated by drafting a "partner-church covenant" that outlines the commitments made. This might include a statement about giving witness to the unity and universality of the body of Christ, a commitment for regular prayer on behalf of the partner church and its ministries, a commitment to correspond and learn from each other, and a commitment to explore ways to encourage one another's ministries and deepen the fellowship between the congregations. The draft covenant can be sent to the partner congregation to revise and, if they so choose, affirm. The covenant should be consecrated in a worship service either prior to sending it or when it is received back from the partner church. The committee, board, or peacemakers group facilitating the partnership could be commissioned to act on behalf of the larger body.

Building and Sustaining the International Partnership

The most convenient way to get the partnership moving and to sustain it over the years is through a regular exchange of letters. The letters can describe topics being presented in sermons or study groups, ministries in which the church is engaged, special milestones in the congregation's life, and some of the concerns that the church members have as they seek to be faithful disciples of Christ. If the partnership is with a congregation speaking a different language, you will probably need someone who can translate their letters for you. Write your letter in their language if at all possible. Many people around the world do know English, but we need to overcome the common assumption that others will accommodate the U.S.'s linguistic ignorance. Making the effort to translate what we say into another's language conveys a deeper message of commitment and respect.

Letters can be sent in packets with other expressions from the church. Children could write letters or draw pictures. Photos of the congregation or groups of people within the church could be sent. A cassette tape of choir music, a sermon, or a church service provides a way for the other congregation to enter into some of your church life. Even recipes can be exchanged. With the use of a speaker phone, you can even arrange for a direct conversation with a member of the partner church during a Sunday service to supplement the communications sent by letter. This takes some advance planning but can be an exciting way to communicate for those who never get the opportunity to travel abroad. The First Baptist Church of Palo Alto has monthly phone conversations with the Primera Iglesia Bautista in Corinto, Nicaragua. A display can be set up in the foyer so that gifts, photos, and letters from the partner church can be seen and read by everyone.

Gifts that express the unity of the congregations can be exchanged. A banner can be made displaying the names of both churches—to be hung in your church for a while, then sent to the partner church. Communion cups or chalices can be sent. One congregation has a glass cup from a Russian partner church that is always mixed in with their own cups to remind the members during the Lord's Supper that they are united with sisters and brothers across the globe. Artists and craftmakers in the congregation could make gifts using their talents: paintings, crocheted wall hangings, embroidered Communion cloths, and the like. A photo album with notes and greetings can be put together.

The congregation can broaden its understanding of the partner church's country through special programs. Speakers from local universities or international students can be invited to discuss the culture and politics of the country. Ask your denominational office when missionaries to that region will be back in the States and visiting your area. The missionaries can share about the country, the ministry of the churches, and perhaps even bring specific greetings from your partner church. The congregation can also learn some liturgical phrases in the language of the partner church as well as a hymn or chorus. Customs about the observance of Christmas and Easter can be printed in the church newsletter or even incorporated into your church's traditional observances.

The partner churches can select certain shared activities, such as observing Human Rights Sunday or World Communion Day, with a focus on their relationship. Sermons can be preached from the same text and then exchanged. Bible study groups can study the same portions of Scripture and then write each other about their reflections and learnings.

As the relationship grows, so does the desire for face-to-face encounters. A group of church members can be sent to visit the partner church, either as a part of a longer tour of the region or specifically to spend time at that church. Arranging for the members to join in a ministry activity and worship service enriches the encounter. Sometimes the partner church can send a pastor or members to visit in the United States; if money is a problem, the U.S. church can invite them to come and pay their expenses. Arrange for the visitors to have opportunities to learn about you and your community as well as to share their concerns and ministries.

Many churches have established relationships with churches from other countries and experienced the joy and broader perspective that comes from connecting to others. The Greece Baptist Church near Rochester, New York, and the Rákoscsaba Baptist Church in Budapest, Hungary, began a partnership from a Baptist Peace Fellowship friendship tour to Eastern Europe in 1988. Paul Hayes, a pastor at Greece Baptist, suggested to the Hungarian pastor, Géza Molnár, that the churches exchange correspondence as a way to improve East-West relations. The correspondence grew to include exchanging gifts, from artwork to embroidery. Videos and audio cassettes of choir music were also sent. One Thanksgiving a couple from the Rákoscsaba church, Ferenc and Margarit Szilágyi, were able to visit Greece Baptist, bringing with them a beautiful Jozsef Toth wood carving of Christ. Throughout the relationship, both congregations have learned about church life in another country and the kinds of issues each body must face in seeking to be faithful to its Christian calling.

The Pullen Memorial Baptist Church in Raleigh, North Carolina, is in a partnering relationship with the First Baptist Church of Matanzas, Cuba. Roger and Mary Ruth Crook from Pullen Memorial have been the key facilitators of the relationship, traveling to Cuba a number of times to speak and participate in worship services.

Our contact with Cuba began when we attended the International Baptist Peace Conference held in Sweden in 1988. There we met Francisco "Paco" Rodes, pastor of the First Baptist Church of Matanzas, Cuba, and Noel Fernández, a layman from Ciego de Avila, Cuba. At our invitation, these two men spent the summer of 1989 living in our home and studying English at the local community college. During that time Paco proposed a sister-church relationship between Pullen and First Baptist of Matanzas to provide contact and mutual support between the two churches. Since that time six groups from our church have visited Matanzas, and five groups from Matanzas have come to Pullen.

Our Cuba mission group meets regularly not only to share our mutual concerns and to pray but also to implement specific activities—some educational, some political, some humanitarian. Pullen has provided significant medical and other material assistance to the Cuban church. More than that, our visits and our prayers have given them spiritual support that they tell us has been life-sustaining.

We, in turn, have gained from them new insight into the meaning of a vital faith, and we have been inspired by their spirit of faithfulness to the mission of the church in the world. Our own worship has been especially enriched by their expressions of faith through music and art. Every visit from our Cuban sisters and brothers has renewed us spiritually and has raised the level of our concern and our commitment to working for reconciliation between our nations. Every member of our congregation who has visited the church in Matanzas has had a truly life-changing experience. Together we have experienced the truth of Paul's affirmation that Christ "has broken down the dividing wall, that is, the hostility between us" (Ephesians 2:14). Our sisters and brothers in Cuba tell us what we already know—that because nothing can separate us from the love of God, neither can anything separate us from the love of one another.

　　　　—Roger and Mary Ruth Crook, Cary, North Carolina

The Tokyo Peace Church in Japan has seen partner churches as a central part of its witness to the reconciling power of the gospel. This Baptist mission church established a partnership with the First Presbyterian Church of Iri, Korea, to address simultaneously the racism in Japan against Koreans and the divisions within the Christian community. Members have visited between the congregations, including five from the Korean church coming to Tokyo to celebrate the formal organizing of the Peace Church following seven years as a mission site. The congregations have exchanged gifts of art and plaques. The Tokyo Peace Church has also established partner churches in India and Oregon.

When John Detwyler returned to Schenectady from Nicaragua, the Emmanuel Baptist church agreed to link up with the Getsemaní Baptist Church. They sponsored a two-week visit of the pastor, Felix Ruíz Rivera, putting together an itinerary that included speaking engagements about life in Nicaragua to churches, colleges, high schools, community and social groups, as well as preaching at Emmanuel. Many of Emmanuel's members have made the trip to visit Getsemaní Baptist in Los Gutiérrez Norte. John and his wife, Sandra George Detwyler, spent a year in Nicaragua as volunteer missionaries, deepening the bonds between the congregations.

Christ has told us to love our neighbor. Sometimes it is difficult for us to connect with each other due to distance, language barriers, and cultural differences; but what we do have in common

---

[1]Sandra George, "Getsemaní Prays for Emmanuel in Every Service . . . ," *PeaceWork*, November/December 1988, 10.

is Christ and a desire for peace and justice, and that overcomes all the other barriers. Our church has grown in an understanding of Christian love through its contact with Getsemaní.
—John Detwyler, Schenectady, New York[1]

Sandra helped establish a sewing collective as an economic development ministry of Getsemaní Baptist Church involving the participation of both congregations. The women from Emmanuel provided the bulk of sewing machines, fabric, thread, and other supplies for the collective. One woman donated five hundred dollars to provide training for the women in the collective. Using her experience as a professional educator, Sandra provided the training and materials for Getsemaní to begin the first free preschool in Los Gutiérrez Norte.

To fund the school for one year, Emmanuel Baptist sponsored two events.

One was a special service in January emphasizing the sister church. Invitations were sent out to those within the community who had verbally and financially supported our ministry in Nicaragua. They included Baptists and laypeople and clergy from other churches: Methodists, Catholics, Unitarians, Lutherans, Presbyterians, and so on. The service was truly ecumenical.

The other event was the "Fiesta de Amistad" (Fiesta of Friendship). Over a hundred people attended the ecumenical fiesta to feast on Cuban black bean soup, Mexican fiesta salad, chile, rice, and brownies. During dinner a Catholic sister visited tables throughout the hall, serenading the "fiesters" with Spanish songs. Following the meal a five-minute slide show was presented telling the story of the preschool, and a sombrero was passed for donations. Later, a Nicaraguan woman danced and the children enjoyed a piñata. Not only was the evening an opportunity to raise funds for the school (over a thousand dollars) but also an opportunity for education.
—Sandra George Detwyler, Schenectady, New York

Financial Paternalism and Gift-Giving

As the congregations learn more about each other and their ministries, the desire may arise in the U.S. church to help out with projects in the partner church, particularly if it is in a poor community.

This can be a legitimate expression of love and unity, but it can also become corrupted by the temptation of financial paternalism. American churches have a lot of money and are even fabulously wealthy by global standards. We tend to think that we can solve problems by giving money. This generosity, at least as we perceive it in ourselves, keeps us from having to acknowledge our own needs and that those we see as poor may have some important contributions to make to us. We can too easily assume that because we have money we should be in control of a relationship.

To counter paternalism in ourselves and dependence in partner congregations, the matter of gift-giving needs to be explicitly confronted. CEPAD, the Protestant relief and development agency in Nicaragua, has helped many U.S. churches link up with Nicaraguan churches. CEPAD insists that no large gifts of money or supplies be made by the U.S. churches in order to keep from falling into a crippling donor-recipient mentality. The partnership needs to be one of equality and mutuality. The U.S. church is not to become an aid or development agency.

Symbolic gifts that express the love and connections between the congregations can be simple and beautiful. More extensive participation in financial aid to development projects can be done more healthily through the national denominational offices or through international organizations. When the First Baptist Church of Ann Arbor, Michigan, wanted to assist their sister church in Nandasmo, Nicaragua, with a poultry-raising project, they worked through the Baptist Convention of Nicaragua. An alternative holiday fair was held at the Ann Arbor church to "donate a chicken," and the funds were given through the Baptist Convention of Nicaragua along established mission-projects channels. Institutional gifts such as seminary scholarships or donations of books to school or seminary libraries are more appropriate than giving money to individuals. In some cases churches will encounter leaders of local ministries who are constantly hustling for financial support. The need may be great, but issues of accountability are often overlooked. From a distance it can be impossible to tell what is fraudulent and what is legitimate. Keeping any significant financial involvement to previously established missions channels will tend to screen out these problems and maintain appropriate accountability.

Building Domestic Church Partnerships

Establishing domestic church partnerships is obviously quite different from international relationships because of the shared community, the opportunities for interaction, and the interwoven histories of churches and neighborhoods. But often there are barriers to be overcome, particularly racism and the social distance it produces. Various ethnic groups can have their own circles in which they move, circles that other groups are unaware of or at least out of touch with. Ministerial alliances can have ethnically homogenous memberships, perhaps not intentionally but through the subtle interactions of racism and varied agendas, needs, and experiences. There is often a track record, for better or worse, of cross-cultural relations in the community, something upon which the domestic church partnership can build if that record is positive.

Call the local offices of the denomination or metropolitan ecumenical organization to see if they have a project in place to link churches. There may be some helpful mechanisms in place for starting relationships. If you are in a smaller setting such as a small city or a neighborhood in which cross-cultural partnerships could be built, the relationship can be started on more personal grounds, such as face-to-face encounters with pastors to explore the idea together. Some peace fellowships have gathered experiences of other churches that can be useful in planning the development of church partnerships. The Baptist Peace Fellowship of North America, for example, has a "Promise of Pentecost" project to encourage churches to overcome the divisions of racism and ethnic alienation. They have resources, Bible studies, and stories from other church partnerships to help get congregations oriented to the challenges and opportunities of such a relationship.

To get the ball rolling, work through the appropriate leadership channels in the church to present the idea and identify the people responsible to pursue it. The people working on the relationship, however, need to be in communication with the whole congregation and have a process through which the entire body is brought into the project and gives its blessing.

Then get to work on building the connection between congregations. Don't be impatient, for friendships are not built hastily, especially if there is a history of racism to be honestly faced. Dr.

David Forbes, Sr., is the former pastor at the Martin Street Baptist Church, an African American congregation paired with the predominately white Pullen Memorial Baptist Church in Raleigh, North Carolina. Dr. Forbes said, "Be aware racism has placed a scar on community central in its making, and no amount of goodwill will eradicate that pattern quickly."[2] Articulate your interest in a partnership with a few specific ideas for acting on the new relationship. Then listen, for the other congregation will need to join in shaping the vision and the structure of the partnership if it is to be a genuine linking together.

The other congregation may have a different time frame in which it approaches the partnership. Establishing the relationship can be very important and feel urgent to you, but the other church may be involved in other areas of mission that relegate the partnership to a lower place on the agenda. They may have internal matters to work through before they can appropriately address the request for a partnership.

It is inevitable that when we go to their meetings, work on their projects, get on their schedule, become concerned with their needs, that we will want to start making changes, to "improve" the way things are done. But it is not ours to change. We are not in control. It is healthy for us to experience being on someone else's agenda.
—Kyle Childress, Nacogdoches, Texas[3]

Patience becomes important, not being put off by a slow response but waiting for the internal workings of the other congregation to move to the point of being able to affirm the decision to pair up.

Pulpit and choir exchanges are the typical starting points for a partnership, and all too often that is as far as matters go. A healthy partnership needs some joint projects in worship and ministry. Special joint services can be held on occasions such as Martin Luther King, Jr.'s birthday, Maundy Thursday or Good Friday, Easter sunrise, Thanksgiving Day, or New Year's Eve. A shared mission project can bring church members together to work side by

---

[2] Paula Womack, "Swimming Upstream Against Racism," *PeaceWork*, May-June/July-August 1990, 11.

[3] Ken Sehested, "How to Start and Sustain a Sister Church Relationship," *PeaceWork*, May-June/July-August 1990, 23.

side, such as vacation Bible school, a housing rehab, or a home weatherization ministry for the poor or elderly church members. Education events can be scheduled together: church-school teacher training, youth-group special activities, or a community issue study and action group. Families can pair up from each church to eat at one another's homes, an idea that was developed by Koinonia Southern Africa to address apartheid at an intimate level.

Besides direct encounters you can make ways to recognize and affirm the unity between the congregations. A joint banner with the names of both congregations can be made and shared back and forth between the churches. Prayers can be regularly offered for the ministry and people of the partner church. Newsletters can carry news from the other congregation, and the key contacts for each congregation should be on the mailing list of the partner church.

We [Underwood Memorial Baptist Church] have paired with Mt. Moriah Baptist Church, an African American congregation located in the Milwaukee central city, for annual shared worship services. On these Sundays, the churches alternate the privilege of serving as host to the two congregations. Choirs from the two churches rehearse together in advance so that they can sing together. The pastor of the guest church brings the morning message while the host church provides a meal for all the worshipers following the service.

We have begun koinonia groups consisting of equal numbers of whites and people of color that covenant for six months to meet for potluck meals in each other's homes to discuss racial/ethnic issues. The groups further agree to complete their covenanted relationship by sharing a meal in a restaurant and some form of public entertainment.

—Reid Trulson, Wauwatosa, Wisconsin

As the relationship grows, the ideas generated can be endless, and they will grow out of the integrity of the relationship and the churches' call and mission. Tough issues will probably emerge; in fact, at some point they *must* emerge if the relationship is to deal honestly with the problems in our society, our churches, and our own selves. A cross-cultural partnership that is genuine will force growth in both congregations and will richly reward those who press ahead to the deeper issues and the unity that can be forged there.

How Far Do You Go?

A church partnership can go as far as the congregations want to take it. Many American churches, especially white churches, have short attention spans, and a church partnership can be a brief mission fad. When a war is going on, churches in countries like Nicaragua can attract our attention, but once the war is over, our attention can easily shift to other places and other issues. But the church in Nicaragua is still there with its struggles and ministries. Domestic relationships can be popular in the wake of racial violence, but racism often slides off the white agenda once superficial law and order is restored, taking the motivation out of cross-cultural relationships for some people.

A periodic reevaluation of the relationship can help congregations take a fresh look at the partnership. There may be a need to shift the focus or risk moving to a new level of involvement. The First Baptist Church in Palo Alto has periodic recommitment services to renew the vision for the partnership. How far a church will go depends on how deep its vision is. A biblically based vision that sees the church as a body of reconciled people will see the issues in partnership as going to the core of the life of the church rather than being mission elective projects. Reconciliation across racial, ethnic, and national lines is Christ's agenda and the Holy Spirit's imperative. Being faithful in working out and maintaining the partnership then becomes an expression of faithfulness to Christ.

Chapter 10

Traveling for Peace

Travel can be a peacemaking ministry when it brings people into face-to-face contact beyond the barriers of national, cultural, or political polarity. When I see the enemy and discover a human being, or when I experience a bit of the life and struggle of someone in a war zone I'd only read about before, my understanding is deepened, my heart is opened, and sometimes my entire life is transformed. Travel can take us out of the confines of our particular community, with its limited perspective of the larger world beyond, and dramatically expand our horizons.

Of course, travel in and of itself isn't peacemaking. Tourists see the sights but often miss the underlying realities. Pilgrims to the Middle East see the old stones of ancient ruins but often miss the "living stones" of people laboring for justice, reconciliation, and peace amid the explosiveness of contemporary politics. Corporate executives jet around the world to improve their company's bottom line, which may aggravate the economic disparities fueling local wars. To be an act of peacemaking, then, travel must have a purpose that shapes the itinerary and the use of the travel experiences.

Many people in our churches travel to other countries for education or ministry. Peace travels can be undertaken to learn about another country, and particularly to visit "the enemy" of our own government. Travel can also be an expression of solidarity with brothers and sisters in difficult situations. Sometimes we can bring them aid or work beside them. We can also listen to their stories and witness their circumstances so that we can return to our own country and give voice to their experiences and concerns.

Traveling with a Peace Purpose

Traveling for peace can have three specific purposes. First, travel can be used to establish relationships. Conflict divides people, whether across international boundaries, embargo lines, or ethnic turf lines in local communities. Going to the other side of the tracks, the expressway, the Iron Curtain, or the Line in the Sand is a way of breaking that isolation. Many church members traveled to the Soviet Union and Eastern Europe during the days of the Cold War to meet people in what some government leaders called the "Evil Empire." Others traveled to Central America to see realities that were not portrayed in the media or accurately conveyed in official government statements. The isolation of hatred, fear, propaganda, and ignorance was overcome.

A second purpose is to witness to our unity in Christ, though our countries may be distant or hostile toward one another. Baptists in the United States and Baptists in Cuba have been reaching out to one another. A group of Baptist women toured Cuba in early 1992 to participate in the ordination of the first woman among Cuban Baptists, expressing solidarity and unity between parts of God's family kept apart by the conflict of political leaders. When the Martin Luther King, Jr., Center, which is sponsored by the Ebenezer Baptist Church in Havana, hosted a youth congress in 1994, youth from Baptist churches in the United States and Puerto Rico attended. Governments rise and fall, policies are developed then changed, but when Christians affirm their unity across the divides of conflict, a deeper reality rooted in the Lord of history is proclaimed.

Sometimes the unity in Christ is expressed as an act of accompaniment with those who suffer. Martin Massaglia, pastor of the Royersford Baptist Church in Pennsylvania, accompanied Salvadoran refugees seeking to return to their home villages after living in camps in Honduras, as a participant in the "Going Home" campaign.

In 1987 a respected member of my congregation [Helen DeLano—see below], at the age of sixty-seven, made a journey to El Salvador as part of a religious delegation. She returned with such passion for helping the poor of El Salvador that before long a large group of us were studying the issues and doing what we could to help from the sidelines. In August 1988 the opportunity came for me to move from words to action by accompanying refugees from a camp in Mesa Grande, Honduras, back to El Salvador. God's call to me was unmistakable, and, before I could even ask my congregation, I had agreed to join a delegation of fifteen people of faith from North America.

Overcoming many obstacles, the disapproval of both the United States and Salvadoran governments, over one thousand brave refugees asserted their right to go home, and it was our privilege to accompany them. It was the most exhilarating, inspiring experience of my entire life. Once informed, my congregation was completely supportive. In fact, they not only paid all my expenses but also sent extra money for the refugees. They supported the repatriation from home by sending telegrams to the Salvadoran government demanding support for the refugees and for the delegation. They also supported us with ongoing prayer and then a two-day prayer vigil during the time of the actual repatriation.

—Martin Massaglia, Royersford, Pennsylvania

Walking with those who suffer is a concrete way of responding to the biblical injunction to "weep with those who weep" (Romans 12:15).

Longer-term partnerships can be developed out of the expressions of Christian unity made by those who cross the political/national divides and join with sisters and brothers, however briefly, in their struggle. Many partner-church relationships have been established as the result of congregation members visiting a church in another country and experiencing a bond that continued after the trip was over. Grace Morgan, a lay leader from the Underwood Baptist Church in Wauwatosa, Wisconsin, visited the Baptist Church on the Marzahner Promenade in East Berlin before the Wall came down. Her initial contact on a Baptist Peace Fellowship friendship tour developed into a partner-church relationship between the two congregations. John Detwyler worked with American Baptist missionaries in Nicaragua for eight weeks in 1985 with the encouragement of his home church, Emmanuel Baptist in Schenectady, New York. While in Nicaragua he visited the village of Los Gutiérrez Norte, where the Getsemaní Baptist Church carried on its ministry. Through John's contact on a volunteer work tour, a partnership grew between the two congregations. Such stories can be told about partnerships that developed after many such trips to various countries.

The third peace purpose of travel is to energize and direct political activism. Traveling to an "enemy" country is a political act itself, as is joining in solidarity with those whose suffering is exacerbated by U.S. policies. Acts of love and expressions of Christian unity are not done in a vacuum but speak with prophetic force. Peacemaking travelers can use their experiences to speak from their own firsthand experiences in advocacy efforts to shape governmental policies and church involvement in advocacy.

Members of our congregation had only begun to learn about the plight of Salvadoran campesinos forced from their homes during the nation's civil war when a call came from a woman gathering a delegation to travel to El Salvador. She wanted to get the real story of what was happening, dialogue with Salvadorans, be a supportive presence at a celebration marking the assassination of Archbishop Romero, and then return and tell the story. Though she had never before done anything like it, and though at sixty-seven years of age some people might have thought it would be too much, Helen DeLano accepted the invitation and made the journey.

Particularly moving to her were the conversations with COMADRES (the mothers of political prisoners, disappeared, and assassinated people of El Salvador). As she experienced both the pain and the inextinguishable hope of the poor, she was, in her own words, "converted again." In the Salvadoran people she saw the suffering Christ manifested in a powerful way. Upon her return she worked tirelessly as an advocate for the sisters and brothers she had left in El Salvador. Whether raising funds and people's consciousness or working in public advocacy for change in our nation's policy related to El Salvador, she was instrumental in making Royersford Baptist Church a major force in the Philadelphia area related to Salvadoran concerns.
—Martin Massaglia, Royersford, Pennsylvania

Thousands of Christians and people of other faiths who traveled to Nicaragua with Witness for Peace delegations could speak to local media and their political representatives from the basis of having seen the *contra* war and its impact directly. One cannot turn away from such an experience unchanged; the people and their stories stay with the peace traveler as an ongoing source of energy and commitment.

Types of Peace Travel

Many travel experiences are organized by groups or agencies outside the local church. A denomination may sponsor a mission work tour. For example, International Ministries of the American Baptist Churches sponsored mission tours of Central America in the 1980s that exposed participants to the problems of life in El Salvador and Nicaragua, to the sorrows of the war, and to the experience of the churches seeking to minister in that context. Various denominations sent teams to South Africa to observe and monitor the 1994 elections. These teams usually included a mix of national staff and people from local churches who had been active in South African issues. Even when individuals within the church sign up to go with such a tour on their own initiative, it can become an opportunity for the entire church to learn, grow, and perhaps act for peace.

Roy and Judy Johnsen both went on denominational tours to Central America. Roy participated in a mission work tour of Costa Rica and Nicaragua in 1982. When he saw the ministry of the churches in the revolutionary society of Nicaragua and saw their suffering at the hands of U.S.-sponsored *contras,* he was moved to greater activism. Upon his return he took every opportunity to speak and lobby for a change in U.S. policy.

In August 1984 I participated in a mission study tour to El Salvador and Nicaragua, sponsored by American Baptist Women. This trip was my first exposure to developing countries and my first exposure to extreme poverty. Both El Salvador and Nicaragua were in the midst of civil wars that were being fought with arms and military aid supplied most extensively from the United States. In both of these countries, people pleaded with our tour group, "Please tell your government

to stop sending military aid. "
   In my naïveté, I had thought that the United States always did the "good" and "right" thing in its relationships with other countries. To realize the amount of suffering, torture, and killing that occurs throughout the world because of arms provided by my country was a painful and eye-opening experience. I realized, as a follow of Jesus Christ, how important it is to work for peace and justice. I realized, as a citizen of the United States, how important it is to express my opinions to my government through correspondence to my senators and representatives.
                       —Judy Johnsen, Williamsport, Pennsylvania

Denominational peace fellowships may also host tours. The Baptist Peace Fellowship of North America was born out of a tour of Southern Baptists and American Baptists to the Soviet Union in 1984. Since then the BPFNA has sponsored "friendship tours" to Eastern Europe, Cuba, Nicaragua, El Salvador, and South Africa, as well as additional tours to the Soviet Union. These tours provide opportunities for learning about the situation in other countries as well as bridge building through the churches.

Peace organizations, and even professional groups, host tours that local church members sometimes join. One church began its involvement in Central American issues when a member of the church who was a school teacher participated in a two-week visit to Nicaragua by educators from their city. Many church folk participated in actions of Witness for Peace or Pastors for Peace, engaging directly in solidarity action by accompanying people in war zones, recording human rights violations, or delivering aid in violation of government-imposed embargoes.

Some trips have been organized within congregations themselves. Members of Central Baptist Church in Wayne, Pennsylvania, have traveled to South Africa and El Salvador to visit partner churches in those countries. Members from Judson Memorial Baptist Church in Minneapolis have traveled to a village in Nicaragua to express their solidarity with a Nicaraguan partner congregation. The First Baptist Church of Greater Cleveland has undertaken an annual mission tour to Nicaragua for twenty-five years. Six to ten people go to Nicaragua for two weeks, working alongside Nicaraguan church members in shared ministry. They find that this regular commitment has broken down barriers between people, created understanding about different ways of life, and given a perspective that can call into question personal lifestyles and national priorities. Because these trips grow out of the mission and social-ministry agendas of the congregations, they give expression to a commitment larger than the interest of only those who go on the trip itself. Youth events can sometimes become peacemaking journeys. International youth conferences, such as those sponsored every five years by the Baptist World Alliance (BWA), expose youth to the diversity of the world community. One youth who went to a BWA conference in Scotland in 1988 was challenged by Third World Baptists about church support of U.S. militarism. His travel encounters led to a dramatic reorienting of his values and social commitments, including changing his involvement in the National Guard because of his new conscientious-objector convictions. Baptist youth from Puerto Rico have participated in work projects with Christians in Cuba, and when the youth congress was held in Havana, Cuba, some American youth attended, crossing the barriers imposed by U.S. hostility and policy. For youth, such travels can be life-transforming encounters with differing people and cultures, even as they are for adults.

Tips for the Peace Traveler

Besides all the regular matters related to travel—documents, shots, itineraries, what to eat and drink—the peace traveler can take a few steps to enhance her or his experience and make a greater impact for peace both in the other country and upon returning home.

Gifts can be taken to tangibly express the peace mission. Plowshares pins (small lapel pins, made of scrap metal from a U.S. fighter plane, depicting a sword being bent into a plow) make easy gifts to carry in quantity.[1] Their vivid symbolism makes them a powerful expression of reconciliation for the traveler crossing into "enemy territory." Roy Johnsen of Williamsport, Pennsylvania, makes beautiful wooden peace ornaments. When I went to the Middle East, I had half a suitcase full of these ornaments to use as gifts for church leaders and congregations I met on my journey. Communion cups or sets have also been used as reconciliation or

---

[1] The pins are available for a modest price from Swords to Plowshares, Box 10406, Des Moines, IA 50306.

solidarity gifts between congregations, leaving tangible expressions of the love and connection that transcends national boundaries and distance.

Recording one's experiences is important to make the most out of peace travel. Tourists have fun and take pictures to treasure their memories (and having to tolerate their pictures has been the source of a fair bit of humor!). A peace traveler, however, has undertaken a mission and has a message to tell. The traveler will encounter people and situations that may be hidden by the ignorance, indifference, or hostility of the government, media, or public back home. So the peace traveler cannot responsibly just take in all that is experienced. There needs to be a time of telling the stories, so the traveler would do well to record them as fully as possible.

Recording the stories can be done in a number of ways. Keeping a journal is a basic discipline that will prove valuable in recalling the people, places, and experiences that can become a confused jumble as you move quickly from one place to the next. Take time each night to record what happened that day, whom you saw, what was said, your impressions and experiences. You can add notes during interviews and documents you pick up to put together a complete log. If there is any risk of your journal being confiscated and used by authorities against dissidents you visit, you should not use names. Either commit the names to memory or write them separately somewhere else, postponing the full reconstruction of your journal until you arrive home.

Taking photographs or videos can always enhance the story you tell when you get home. Be sure to ask people if you can take a picture or a video before you begin shooting. People are not objects for our ideological use, so show basic human respect and courtesy to the people you encounter. Slides or edited videos can help those in your home church or those who attend a presentation on your trip get a bit more of a feel of what you encountered and the people you met. When members of the peacemakers group at Dorchester Temple Baptist in Boston saw a slide show about a visit to El Salvador, seeing the pictures of children leaving their outdoor school class to climb into the crude bomb shelter during an attack brought home the horror of the bombing campaign in that country's civil war more than all the general statements of how bad it was.

The stories of people from another country are more powerful in conveying the realities of their lives and the passions of their concerns than statistics or recitations of history and political relations. Hearers of a presentation can relate more readily to the stories of named individuals with whom they can identify. The death of thirty thousand people reported in a newspaper will not move the heart as much as the story of a mother who told the group about losing three children in the war. The personal story of one black friend's daily ordeals living under apartheid in South Africa gave a personal angle to a national experience that revealed the core of that larger reality more than any general statements ever could. So make special note of the stories while they are fresh in your mind because these stories are what you will remember most vividly from your travels.

Involving the Congregation

Those in the congregation who do not go on the trip can still share in the peacemaking venture of the one who travels. Participating in sending the traveler can both link that traveler into the community of the church as well as hold him or her accountable to report back upon return. The one who travels is not going on his or her own but is sent as a representative, as a citizen ambassador.

International travel is expensive, and help in raising funds for the trip is one simple but extremely practical way a congregation can support a peace journey. Fund-raising support can enable people of more limited means but a deep peacemaking commitment to go on trips they could never make otherwise. It also allows people who cannot make the trip to express their support of the peace mission by helping to finance it.

Fund-raising in the church also provides an opportunity to educate the church members and the community about the issue. When church folks go on Witness for Peace delegations, a fund-raising event is an occasion where the conflict, whether in Nicaragua, Guatemala, or Mexico, can be highlighted. Aspects of the conflict that don't make the national news can be brought to people's attention with the assurance that they can help someone they know gain some firsthand experience about what is happening.

When the person or group goes, a commissioning service can be a moving experience for all involved. When Andy Smith went to

South Africa as an observer of the 1994 elections, his home church took time in their Sunday morning worship to commission him.

> *A number of colored ribbons hung from the large cross above the center of the sanctuary that Sunday. I was sitting under a ribbon of a different color. Steve Jones, the pastor, asked the children to find the special person and then asked them why I was special. He explained that I was about to go to South Africa to observe the elections. At the close of his story about the elections, Steve invited all the children to lay their hands on me as he prayed. I felt the presence and blessing of God and everyone in the congregation that day through the children. During the two weeks in South Africa, I sensed a calmness in myself that I rarely had on previous trips. I knew that the children and indeed the whole congregation were with me in spirit and were praying for my safety as well as a peaceful and successful election.*
>
> —*J. Andy Smith, Wayne, Pennsylvania*

There is a bonding created at such moments that increases the interest and commitment of all involved.

While the travelers are gone, they should be remembered during the congregational prayers each Sunday. If they are visiting a partner church, symbols of that partnership could be prominently displayed at the front of the sanctuary to keep all the members aware of the current connection between the distant congregations.

As mentioned earlier, gifts from the congregation give tangible expression abroad of a community back in this country that shares the concerns expressed by the traveling peacemaker. Before George Williamson, a member of the First Baptist of Granville, Ohio, traveled to Iraq just prior to the outbreak of the Gulf War, he took Polaroid photos of all the children at his church. He got an opportunity to give the photos to children in Bagdad, helping create a visible tie between First Baptist's children and the Iraqi children who would soon be under American bombardment.[2]

Upon their return an opportunity should be made for the peace travelers to report. This could be a few minutes in a service, or even

---

[2] The amazing story of how George Williamson distributed the photos is recorded in full in my book *Christian Peacemaking: From Heritage to Hope* (Valley Forge, Pa.: Judson Press, 1994), 102.

a sermon. A church school class or coffee-hour forum could give an opportunity for a fuller report, including slides and videos. Special presentations could be set up to which the community is invited as well, broadening the scope of reporting on the trip as well as giving witness to the church's concern for peace issues. People should be encouraged to respond to the report or presentation if possible. Those who traveled to Nicaragua often provided letter-writing materials so that church members could write Congress about upcoming *contra*-aid votes. People who traveled to South Africa provided material about the Shell boycott, since Shell was a major corporate supporter of the apartheid regime. Providing an opportunity for a response turns the travel experience into an advocacy education event. It also enables the traveler to keep a commitment of solidarity made to those visited during the trip.

Making the Most of the Media

Before and after an international trip, you can use the media to tell your story and express your concerns to the larger community in which you live. Whereas a report to one's home church might draw twenty to fifty people, getting the story in a local paper can reach twenty thousand or fifty thousand readers—or more. You are newsworthy because your trip relates to issues of national concern while also providing a local connection. Your firsthand experience provides the local media a close-to-home source for information as well as a connection to people in the local community. Contacting a reporter with your story is not an intrusion. You are not bothering the press but are helping them get their job done, particularly if you present clearly what is going on and why this is of interest to the community.

Before going on an international peace trip, consider carefully a plan to utilize the media so that you can have the greatest possible impact at home.[3] Most U.S. citizens have little knowledge of the

---

[3]G. W. Associates has produced an excellent one-hour cassette tape workshop entitled "Living Media." It discusses in detail how to effectively use your local media in relation to travel to the Third World for peace, justice, or ecological purposes. "Living Media" is available at a nominal price from G. W. Associates, 702 S. Beech, Syracuse, NY 13210 (315-476-3396). This tape is highly recommended as an important part of preparation for international peace travel.

Third World—and what they do have is often limited to stereotypes or seen through the filters of U.S. policy and national media, which generally tends to reflect that policy. When the perspective of the peacemaking community is in opposition to U.S. policy, such as was the case in the wars in Nicaragua and El Salvador, then local peacemakers need to use their hometown media to convey the perspectives usually screened out before reaching the public. Your peace work connected with the peacemaking journey is not over until you have tried to involve the local media.

To begin, make a profile of yourself and others in the group for the media to use. This includes a biographical sketch, your occupation, professional and community associations, interests, and so on.

Then identify the media in your area. Print media include the various papers, large city and Sunday editions, and suburban and specialty papers such as minority and religious papers. As you look at the unions, professional associations, or alumni groups with which the travelers are affiliated, consider which might be interested in an article for their newsletter. Also identify the broadcast media, both radio and television. What news programs and talk shows may have an interest? Remember the special angles you might have to interest religious stations or college and university stations. You can find information and phone numbers from the Yellow Pages or from your local library.

Next, you have to make your contacts. Call the papers to talk to reporters who might be interested in the story. Explain why it is important and interesting and what the local connections are to the national and international story. Provide background on yourself, the country, and the issues with which you are concerned. If you have identified someone at the news desk, you could send a press release first, but then follow up with a phone call. Contact producers at radio and television stations with the same information. It is wise to keep detailed records of whom you have contacted and what you have discussed or sent to them.

Make these contacts well in advance of departure—at least two weeks. Stories can be done before you even go that focus on who is going, the purpose of the trip, what you expect to find and do, and whether any collections are being taken for materials or funds. For example, when the Pastors for Peace caravans are put together, local publicity has helped raise awareness of the materials being collected for shipment to Nicaragua or Cuba. Advance publicity helps people who may not be in your network's communication loop learn what is going on so they can participate as well. When you return, you can tell about your experiences and educate others about the situation and U.S. policy related to it. You can make your pictures, slides, and videos available to enhance the story or interview. You can also ask if the paper or station is interested in a particular story or angle. You could offer to do an editorial or a feature story yourself for their consideration.

Prepare for an interview so that you will say what you want to say. Identify specifically the issues that are important to cover. Think through the kind of language and choice of words that will best convey your concerns to your audience. Identify the particularly compelling stories of people you met. Think through the experiences on the trip that made their deepest impression on you: What made them significant? What did you feel? If you are on radio or television, let your feelings animate your voice; a monotonous speaking voice will turn off a listener fairly fast. Once a story is run, follow up with a thank-you to the reporter, producer, or editor involved. Politely correct any points that aren't accurate. Remember that you may need to come back again with another story; you are building a relationship. Appreciation for the work done by the media will help build a cooperative spirit, which will be needed the next time you have a peacemaking story to tell.

Chapter 11

Money and Social Stewardship

Money is a primary link in social relationships all around the world, even for people who never meet one another. Because of the interrelatedness of the global economy, issues of money link us either to conflicts and unjust situations or to creative solutions to conflicts, whether we are aware of it or not. Peacemakers need to recognize the stewardship opportunities related to finances so that our money becomes a tool for building peace rather than sustaining violence.

The stewardship of our money for peacemaking can be a corporate matter for the church, as the congregation looks at its financial and physical resources and the role they can play as investments or mission contributions. Our personal finances and how we spend our money can also have an impact in the congregation. What we do with our money can have legal implications as well, such as when the church is paying someone involved in tax resistance. All these matters will be examined in this chapter in the context of being good stewards of our resources and making the most of them for peace.

Peaceful Church Budgets

The two major ways the church budget can be a vehicle for peacemaking are mission contributions and investments. Contributions from the church budget to organizations working for peace deliver a clear statement about the congregation's understanding of peacemaking as a part of the calling of God's people. Many denominations have peace offices to which gifts can be given. The Presbyterian Church (U.S.A.) has an annual Peacemaking Offering that is used to fund the national work of their Peacemaking Program as well as to support local peace initiatives. There are also grassroots peace fellowships with denominational affiliations, such as the Baptist Peace Fellowship of North America[1] or New Call to Peacemaking[2] for the historic peace churches. Even a small annual contribution from a congregation is appreciated by such peace fellowships, and once the organization is in the budget, it tends to stay in for a while. Other organizations dealing with peace issues, either globally or locally, are always deeply appreciative when a local church makes a donation to their work. The identification and support of the church provides affirmation in what can often be a difficult and controversial witness made by such organizations.

A member desiring to get a peacemaking ministry into the church budget needs to know the process for developing and approving the budget. The appropriate committee, board, or person should be contacted with the request to consider the particular peace group. Supporting materials should be readied and presented to those making the decision. If the organization is accepted in the budget, either the person suggesting the contribution or the appropriate committee in the church should publicize the work of the peace group and its connection to the congregation's own ministry. There may also be programmatic ways in which the congregation can share in the work of the peace group so that the partnership goes beyond a monetary contribution. Newsletters can be displayed on literature tables, and action projects for the fellowship or peace organization can be taken on as congregational projects. Such a partnership gives greater significance to the financial partnership.

Investing for Peace and Justice

Investments are more complex than mission contributions. If a church has endowed funds, the trustees or financial officers usually

---

[1] 499 S. Patterson, Memphis, TN 38111.
[2] P.O. Box 500, Akron, PA 17501.

have the responsibility to oversee the investment of those funds so that income is gained for the church. But the investment itself can be a ministry. Often such funds are deposited in banks or with brokers for the purpose of maximizing the return within certain constraints for security of the investment. But when investments are made for financial reasons alone, the money can be used for purposes that are antithetical to the values and goals of the gospel. For example, the broker could invest in stock in a weapons manufacturer that gains its profits by selling arms to poor countries, thus fueling wars that destroy decades of mission work in the wake of their chaos. Furthermore, the manufacture of weapons may be polluting our own communities. So the net result is that the church has made money off the misery of the poor in the developing world and the degradation of the environment at home. This is both bad stewardship and ethical irresponsibility.

Using investments as a form of congregational ministry, however, can open doors of peacemaking that many church members have never imagined before. Trustees can become agents in an exciting work for impacting the world with gospel values on behalf of the entire congregation. J. Andy Smith, in his book *God's Gift, Our Responsibility,*[3] speaks of three different approaches to corporate responsibility related to investments: positive, negative, and activist. The negative approach is to avoid investments in companies that do business in areas the church does not wish to support. For example, some congregations or denominations will not invest in corporations that are involved in military production. During the struggle against apartheid in South Africa, many churches barred their brokers from investing church funds in companies doing business in that country.

The positive approach involves putting the money to direct use in ventures that are in line with mission goals. Putting church deposits in a minority bank can help strengthen poor communities and undergird local economic development and efforts for racial

---

[3]J. Andy Smith, *God's Gift, Our Responsibility: Biblical Reflections on Creation, Christian Stewardship and Corporate Responsibility* (Valley Forge, Pa.: National Ministries, 1993), 69-74.

justice.[4] Many churches banded together in Philadelphia to help establish the United Bank. They encouraged their members to invest in the bank so that their money would be engaged in the ministry of economic development in some of the city's poorer communities. Some churches also bought stock directly in the bank. In Detroit, church involvement in economic development in partnership with a local bank is taking place as several Detroit congregations have invested in the First Independence National Bank, an African American bank committed to building up the community. The Pax World Fund is a common stock mutual fund established by a group of Methodists to provide alternatives to investments in defense corporations.[5] Opening accounts in such institutions means your church's checking account or investment portfolio can be doing ministry even while waiting for the treasurer to apply the funds to other areas of ministry.[6]

Investments in community development loan funds can be riskier since they aren't insured, but they also help organizations that are addressing the root causes of war and violence. These loan funds often have excellent payback records, but even when the return is lower than standard investments, the social payback is very high. The Alternative Investment Clearing House of the Interfaith Center for Corporate Responsibility[7] provides information about groups and organizations for such alternative investments. There are also social investment funds that operate like traditional brokers but buy

---

[4] One of the most successful community development banks is the South Shore Bank of Chicago. The bank developed Shorebank Advisory Services to help community leaders concerned about economic justice evaluate the needs of their own communities. Shorebank Advisory Services will consult about beginning a process to recapitalize areas that receive little in the way of banking services or investment incentives. A church must be committed for the long haul if it intends to get involved in economic development because genuine solutions are long-term and require hard work. For more information, contact Shorebank Corporation, 71st at Jeffrey Blvd., Chicago, IL 60649-2400 (312-288-1000 or 312-288-2400).

[5] Contact the Pax World Fund at 224 State St., Portsmouth, NH 03801 (603-431-8022). A socially responsible money market fund is available through Working Assets, 111 Pine St., San Francisco, CA 94111 (800-223-7010).

[6] For an extensive listing of investment alternatives, see Appendix C in J. Andy Smith's *God's Gift, Our Responsibility*.

[7] 475 Riverside Dr., Rm. 566, New York, NY 10115.

stock in corporations involved in the manufacture of socially and environmentally positive products, such as alternative fuels, recycled materials, and so on.

The activist approach takes a bit more work and must be done in partnership with other groups. Many denominations have offices that are responsible for the denomination's relations to corporations, such as the Social and Ethical Responsibility in Investments Program for the American Baptist Churches.[8] These offices often use shareholder resolutions to call on corporations to act in socially and environmentally responsible ways. From 1971 to 1993 the religious community led an effort to use shareholder resolutions calling for companies to divest themselves of their business enterprises in South Africa as part of the global campaign to end apartheid. Shareholder resolutions have been used to call for acceptance of a code of environmental ethics, for a halt to nuclear weapons production, for an end to the production of war toys, and the reporting of foreign arms sales, to name a few.

Many churches will let their investment bankers or trustees vote their shares for them, which could result in votes being made in opposition to the peacemaking goals of the congregation. The church can ask that the proxy statements from the corporations for their annual meetings be sent directly to the church for them to vote through their own committee or selected individual. The congregation could also contact the denominational offices, perhaps adding their shares to the shares voted as a block by the denomination. The Central Baptist Church of Hartford, Connecticut, has been a sponsoring shareholder with National Ministries of the American Baptist Churches for several years.

Our church voted to invest in support of the antiapartheid movement in South Africa. We felt we had to get a mandate from the congregation, so a resolution was passed. The motivation for this change came from Central's Board of Outreach. They had undertaken a campaign to write to companies listed within our stock portfolio. They urged support of the Sullivan Principles and asked for information on South African policy. The board also urged the trustees to communicate with Andy Smith (of the Home Mission Society—National Ministries for the

---

[8] National Ministries, P.O. Box 851, Valley Forge, PA 19482-0851.

American Baptist Churches) on the proposed policy change,
which resulted in the final resolution for the American Baptist
Home Mission Society to represent Central Baptist Church of
Hartford in the filing of shareholder resolutions.
                          —Fred Falcone, Hartford, Connecticut

Each year Central Baptist of Hartford sends the list of their stock to the director of Social and Ethical Responsibility in Investments so that their stocks can be added into the denomination's proposals in shareholder meetings. The church simply sends a letter authorizing the church agency or official to act on its behalf and agrees not to sell the stock until after the annual shareholder meeting. A church trustee also sends an authorization of ownership. If many other congregations with endowed funds would join Central Baptist of Hartford, the impact of the denomination's corporate witness would be magnified.

Frequently there are so many corporate meetings going on in the spring that denominational staff cannot attend them all. In that case volunteers from a local church could attend on behalf of all the shareholders in the denominational action and vote at the annual meeting on the issue in question. Pastors or laypeople interested in participating in such action can contact their denominational office related to corporate responsibility and offer their services. If a shareholder meeting is being held within driving distance, then the local church member can play an important role in partnership with national staff.

To engage in such investment peacemaking, the congregation's financial leadership might need to study the matter together, looking at both the biblical issues and the financial options. Andy Smith's *God's Gift, Our Responsibility* provides a series of biblical reflections to help the congregation's financial decisions be grounded in a sound theological and ethical base. The book also provides practical direction to enable a congregation to begin revamping its investment practices. Once the finance committee or trustees are clear about what they intend to do and why, their reasoning and decisions should be presented to the congregation. This will allow fuller ownership of the peaceful and just stewardship of congregational resources, as well as educate the broader membership of the implications and opportunities of stewardship.

Wills, Bequests, and Memorials

Wills and bequests allow individuals to continue their ministry beyond their own lifespans. Such special gifts can be used to open up new peacemaking opportunities both for churches and for national bodies. Victor and Eileen Gavel gave the money to initiate the Edwin T. Dahlberg Peace Award for the American Baptist Churches (ABC). The award is given at the denominational conventions and is named after one of the great peacemakers in the life of the ABC. After years of underwriting the award, when the Gavels had both died, their will left sufficient funds to continue the award indefinitely.

Part of financial discipleship work in a congregation is instructing people how to use their wills to further the purposes of God. A congregation can hold a seminar on making wills. People can be encouraged to give to the endowment of the church or to help initiate or support special ministries in the congregation, including peace projects. Members can also be instructed as to how they can give to mission agencies and peace organizations to further these ministries as well. When Victor Gavel died, he also left money to the Baptist Peace Fellowship of North America, which was used to upgrade their administrative capacity through the purchase of new computer equipment and to inaugurate a new peace fund to support indigenous peace initiatives around the world.

Memorials can also be a way in which a person's death can provide an opportunity for inspiration and growth in peace work. Two deceased members of the Emmanuel Baptist Church in Ridgewood, New Jersey, had been inspirations to the members of that church throughout their long lives of service to Christ and the cause of peace. The church established a peace lounge as a memorial to Carl Tiller and Marie Stites. The lounge contains a library on pacifism and is used for lectures and discussions as well as for meditation and reading. Setting up a memorial that carries on such work is an appropriate and lasting way to honor a deceased peacemaker. Memorials that enable further peace witness also connect the past and the future in a way that adds meaning and strength to both.

The Church Building As a Peacemaking Resource

Many church buildings have plenty of unused or underused space. Such space offers an opportunity for ministry. Most peace-and-justice organizations operate on minimal budgets and are sometimes so hard-pressed financially that staff go without pay. A congregation can provide office space to organizations consistent with the church's mission goals at low rent, no rent, or the cost of utilities.

Agreements to lease church facilities to a tenant organization should be drawn up in writing, clearly delineating space use, restrictions, and financial provisions. This will help both the tenant group and the church avoid unnecessary conflicts down the road. A church board or staff person should be designated as the liaison between the congregation and the tenant organization.

Some churches have housed many organizations on their premises. The Prescott Memorial Baptist Church in Memphis houses offices of a number of groups, including the Baptist Peace Fellowship of North America. Central America Mission Partners is located at the First Baptist Church in Oakland, California. Old Cambridge Baptist Church in Cambridge, Massachusetts, has provided space for many of the leading peace-and-justice groups in the Boston area over the years. The churches benefit from the stimulation and connections provided by these organizations as well as receiving some modest income from rents. The tenant groups benefit by having affordable facilities and sometimes by sharing office equipment such as copiers.

At times there can be a cost to housing peace-and-justice organizations. During the height of the wars in Central America in the mid-1980s, U.S. peace groups were often targets of break-ins and vandalism. The Pledge of Resistance offices in the Old Cambridge Baptist Church were repeatedly ransacked. Answering machines were stolen on the eve of demonstrations, thus removing messages to inform callers about the upcoming events. Files were riffled and tossed around the office. Though repeated complaints were filed, no investigation was undertaken about what appeared to be politically motivated crimes. Sanctuary churches (see chapter 14) also experienced this type of harassment. A church that opens its doors to a group challenging violence or injustice needs to know of potential costs for providing hospitality and be willing to stand in solidarity if necessary.

Spending Money Justly

A congregation can encourage and facilitate people to spend money in ways that contribute to justice. Much of the injustice in the world is rooted in the inequities in the distribution of wealth, the production of goods and services, and the payment for those goods and services. Creative programming can present opportunities for redistributing wealth from more well-to-do U.S. congregations by paying poor craftmakers appropriately for their work.

The Central Baptist Church in Wayne, Pennsylvania, runs the Crafts of Freedom Shop with church volunteers. The shop, located in the church's Mission House, sells craft items made by poor persons from around the world. During the civil rights struggle of the 1960s, several women at Central Baptist, while looking for a way to make a contribution to peace and justice, identified a need for an outlet for the craft and food products made by persons in low-income areas of the United States and Third World. They opened the Crafts of Freedom Shop and operated it completely by volunteers. All profits from the shop go to help groups and co-ops develop new products or expand their markets.

> *Currently among our sources for products are SELFHELP of the Mennonite Central Committee; SERVE of the Church of the Brethren; Thai Tribal Crafts, related to the American Baptist Churches; Koinonia Farms in Americus, Georgia; Berea College Industries, Kentucky; and UNICEF. Twenty-eight years later customers still appreciate the opportunity to purchase a quality product while at the same time helping someone to be freed from the cycle of poverty. The shop is open every day, October through December, and several days each month, January through May.*
> *—Bud Wilmot, Kennett Square, Pennsylvania*

The Valley Forge Presbyterian Church in King of Prussia, Pennsylvania, has sponsored alternative Christmas fairs. The fair features craft items from Third World cooperative outlets and information about various economic development missions. A person can give a gift to buy ten trees for a reforestation project in the Dominican Republic, ducks for a farmer in war-torn Mozambique, or trees to restore an orchard in Lebanon. Local projects such as Habitat for Humanity or battered-women's shelters also have tables where people can buy gifts to assist in building homes or rebuilding shattered lives.

Church newsletters can publicize nonprofit marketing organizations for Third World craftmakers, particularly at Christmas. The materialism of much of the Christmas celebrations can be countered with an opportunity to give gifts that provide a more just form of income distribution. Pueblo to People supports craft and agricultural cooperatives of the poor in Central America and the Philippines.[9] The Mennonite Central Committee has a project, SELFHELP Crafts of the World, which supplies both nonprofit shops and local groups doing short-term craft sales or running a mail-order catalog.[10]

Tax Resistance

"Render to Caesar the things that are Caesar's, and to God the things that are God's," Jesus said (Mark 12:17, RSV). For most people this means individuals should simply pay their taxes in line with the laws of the land. But some Christians see war-making and the destruction of human life as an illegitimate activity of Caesar. To pay taxes for war is, in good conscience, to violate God's call, according to these conscientious objectors. From this concern has grown a national movement of tax resistance that has taken many forms. It has also promoted a legislative campaign to pass the U.S. Peace Tax Fund Bill, which would allow taxpayers to designate their taxes exclusively for nonmilitary use.[11]

Tax resistance could be viewed as a purely individual matter, but the local congregation can and perhaps even must face the issue in two ways. If individuals in the congregation are involved in tax

---

[9] For a catalog, contact Pueblo to People, 2105 Silber, Suite 101, Houston, TX 77055 (800-843-5257).

[10] For a catalog or information, contact SELPHELP Crafts of the World, 704 Main St., P.O. Box 500, Akron, PA 17501 (717-859-4971).

[11] For information, write the National Campaign for a Peace Tax Fund, 2121 Decatur Pl., NW, Washington, DC 20008.

resistance, it would be appropriate to provide an opportunity for them to present what they are doing and the biblical, ethical, and political basis for their decision to act in disobedience to the government. The biblical passages in Mark 12:13-17 and Romans 13:1-7 can be discussed, along with other passages on the themes of peace and government authority. Materials about the U.S. Peace Tax Fund Bill can be made available for people who wish to write their legislators, whether or not they are directly engaged in tax resistance.

In some cases tax resistance can be an issue brought to a congregation because of actions of an employee, particularly a pastor, though anyone in the employ of a church could engage in tax resistance. Nonclergy employees usually have their taxes taken out by the church, and the treasurer sends the withheld money to the Internal Revenue Service. An employee engaged in tax resistance may file for a refund for military taxes paid or choose to reduce his or her income by charitable contributions, which would not impinge on the church itself. If the employee requests that no taxes be withheld, the church is liable to IRS penalties. A pastor, however, is considered self-employed for tax purposes, so no tax is withheld. The clergyperson controls the tax resistance, and IRS collection from the church becomes more difficult.

Dick Myers, pastor of the West Henrietta Baptist Church near Rochester, New York, and his wife, Beth, engaged in tax resistance in the mid-eighties. They sold a home from a prior pastorate and withheld the portion of the capital gains tax that would have gone to the military. The Myers told their pastoral relations committee and other members of the church what they were doing because one of the main purposes of their tax resistance was to make a public witness. One member was concerned that the church not be asked to pay the Myers' taxes for them, but generally the members were supportive. The main church board was also supportive of their pastor doing whatever he felt in conscience he should do, seeing it as not an issue for the church itself. The IRS ended up dealing directly with the Myers by seizing personal assets but not involving the church.

Charles Hurst was involved in tax resistance with his wife, Maria Smith, while pastoring Bethany Presbyterian Church in Cleveland.

The IRS twice sent a levy to the church demanding that Hurst's salary be turned over to pay taxes and penalties. The first time, the church went through a serious discussion among the session, the church's governing board, and the entire congregation. They decided to honor the levy, but sent a letter of support for their pastor's tax resistance to the IRS. They also organized a supportive ecumenical service to make the matter a public one. The second levy, following Hurst's continued tax resistance, was met with refusal to comply. The congregation sent a letter stating their reasons to the IRS. The IRS made numerous threats, but the church continued to refuse to comply with the levy. Rev. Hurst left the church to work with Witness for Peace in Central America. After a year the Justice Department informed the church that legal action against the church was imminent. Legal advisors said the church would not be allowed to give the reasons for its stand; the judge would only consider whether or not the church complied with the levy. To save further expense, the church complied with the levy. Throughout the process Rev. Hurst and his wife felt supported by the congregation both personally and in their beliefs about tax resistance.[12]

The historic peace churches have had more experience with tax resistance and its institutional implications. The Mennonite Church and the General Conference Mennonite Churches have passed resolutions on the issue supportive of individual conscience. Employees of church agencies who have taxes withheld have engaged in resistance by increasing their W-4 withholding allowances. Though the IRS has requested payment to be made by agencies garnishing wages, the agencies have refused. As of this writing, no further action has been taken against the institutions, but individuals have had accounts frozen and liens placed on property. Most churches who have been approached by the IRS have referred the IRS back to the pastor involved in the resistance. There are many church/state issues entangled here, and the IRS seems unwilling to push the matter.

---

[12] Charles Hurst's story is found in "Silence and Courage: Income Taxes, War and Mennonites, 1940-1993" by Titus Peachey, MCC Occasional Paper No. 18, Mennonite Central Committee, August 1993. Many other instances of tax resistance and religious bodies are recounted along with a history of tax resistance and Mennonite individual and denominational actions.

Chapter 12

A Ministry of Advocacy

As a democracy, the United States depends on its citizens to shape the direction and decisions of the country. From Moses addressing Pharaoh and Daniel speaking to Nebuchadnezzar, God's people have acted on the assumption that government leaders are to be held accountable to do what is right and just. In a democracy, however, the government leaders are constitutionally accountable to the people. Not only is there a prophetic ministry of speaking to those in power; there is a ministry of advocacy. Advocacy means getting involved in the dialogue that shapes government decisions and speaking out for one's values and concerns. An advocate makes a case for a particular position and then presses that case to those who make the decision. Since in a democracy our government officials are either elected by us or appointed by those whom we elect, they are ultimately accountable for our concerns. If they do not effectively represent those concerns, we can vote them out of office.

Churches involved in peacemaking have a ministry of advocacy because what happens in our world is of concern to God. God is not neutral about matters that affect human beings. We may not understand fully what God wants, sometimes claiming God is on our side when we may be the ones with the distorted perspective. But for what we do see and do understand, we can advocate. Advocacy is a form of ministry when it is flowing out of our faith and is seeking to make a constructive difference in the world. As ministry it has a place in the work of the church.

But what about the separation of church and state? The separation of church and state is a fundamental principle of Baptist heritage and is embodied in the First Amendment of the U.S. Constitution. The separation of church and state does not mean that religious people cannot express their values in the political discourse of a democracy. After all, everyone has some sort of value system, and for religious people that value system is rooted in faith. All politics involve values, so religious people should be expected to bring their religious/ethical perspectives into the debate and decision-making process.[1]

The separation of church and state means that it is inappropriate for the state to use its power and resources to promote any particular religious group or to promote religion in general. Religious people are citizens in the democracy, but religious institutions are not to be dependent on the government for their support. Such support would involve coercion of conscience on religious matters, something that Baptists have historically resisted for themselves and for others. On the other hand, no church should be permitted to exercise political power in the government or dictate government policy. Yet individual people of faith and religious organizations and institutions can make their voices heard in public debate on government policies and programs in the same way nonreligious citizens and organizations do.

Practically speaking, this means that a local congregation should not expect or seek government support of its religious life, whether in the form of money, religious school tuition credits, or public support of religious practices. Churches should expect that the government will not interfere with their own expression of faith, including evangelistic outreach and works of ministry to those in

---

[1]"A Shared Vision: Religious Liberty in the 21st Century" is a cogent document signed by an extensive interfaith list of religious leaders and organizations on the relationship of religion and politics in the United States. It explores the separation of church and state in constitutional terms and court interpretations, with specific application to some of the pressing current religious liberty issues. "A Shared Vision" is available along with a study guide from the Baptist Joint Committee, 200 Maryland Ave., NE, Washington, DC 20002 (202-544-4226; fax: 202-544-2094).

need. Furthermore, the church can encourage individual members to speak out on political issues from moral and ethical grounds, as well as speaking corporately either as a local congregation or as a regional or national body.

Organizing for Advocacy

Some people in the congregation will write their legislators on their own, but the advocacy ministry of the local church can be dramatically increased by some simple organizing. This can be done without creating any new group but by having an established group act as the catalyst for the larger body. Often one person in the group will be the driving force, providing the information and enlisting a few others in the process.

A Sunday school class, mission action group, peacemakers group, or even the deacons can be the facilitating group. They should do their homework about the issue. If the denomination has any policy statement or resolution on the topic, it would be helpful to secure copies from the headquarters.[2] These resolutions and statements can give members an understanding of positions taken by the representatives of the denomination's churches from across the country as well as some of the theological rationale for the positions. Particular legislative issues and voting timetables can be obtained through the various offices and coalitions in Washington, D.C., or in similar organizations in the state capitals for regional issues.

Advocacy training can be done in the facilitating group or opened up to the congregation at large. This could be handled in a one-session class. A video on advocacy could be shown.[3] A presentation could be made about how to write and visit your legislators and how bills become law.

---

[2] For the American Baptist Churches, contact the Office of Issue Development, National Ministries, P.O. Box 851, Valley Forge, PA 19482.

[3] An excellent advocacy training video is *Advocacy Is a Ministry*, available for rental or purchase from the ABC Office of Governmental Relations, 110 Maryland Ave., NE, Washington, DC 20002 (202-544-3400) or from National Ministries Literature Resources, P.O. Box 851, Valley Forge, PA 19482 (800-458-3766). The Office of Governmental Relations also has an annually updated booklet available at a nominal fee called "Register Citizen Opinion: A Congressional Directory and Action Guide."

Once the facilitating group is clear about the issue, the specific legislation, and the time frame for action, plans can be made to either act as a small group or to present the action opportunity to the entire congregation. In the latter case, an announcement can be made with a brief statement of the issue and why the church members are being encouraged to act. Then an opportunity needs to be made for immediate response. A table can be set up in the narthex, foyer, or coffee-hour lounge. The action table should have information sheets, a sample letter, stationery, pens, envelopes, and stamps.

Of course, to prevent unnecessary conflict in the congregation, the facilitating group should take its request to set up an advocacy table to the appropriate leadership body or church board. Avoid partisan politics, keeping the focus on the ethical concerns that are at stake in the legislative decisions.

The comments in this chapter are primarily about advocacy at a national level, but peace and justice need advocates locally as well. Often local peace-and-justice issues are clouded by seemingly mundane matters such as zoning, administration, civil service, and the like. However, the implications of decisions amid the details of state, city, and county governments can be immense for the quality of people's lives and the conditions of local communities. The same basic characteristics of effective advocacy apply locally as nationally: do your homework, know your issue, build relationships with officials, be respectful but also clear about where you stand. There are more opportunities to build relationships with local politicians and government officials than with national, so an active congregation advocating for justice and peace can be a significant player in the discussions shaping issues of local policy.

How to Write Effective Letters

In a survey of congressional staffpersons about the types of communications to which members of Congress respond, the number-one answer was spontaneous constituent mail.[4] Letters to representatives

----

[4] "Register Citizen Opinion 1993: A Congressional Directory & Action Guide," General Board of Church and Society of the United Methodist Church, 3. Available from Service Department, General Board of Church and Society, 100 Maryland Ave., NE, Washington, DC 20002 (202-488-5600).

and senators as well as state and local officials are an important channel to get one's voice heard and to help shape decisions. Since less than one in ten citizens write their Congresspeople, the impact of each letter is significant. Petitions are not a very effective means of advocacy; letters make a far greater impact. A postcard is not as effective as a letter, but a handwritten postcard is better than nothing or than a preprinted postcard.

In writing a letter, be sure to put your address on the letter itself since envelopes are thrown away. It is best to be brief, keeping your focus on a single issue. A letter of several pages will probably not be carefully read, so be concise and well organized in your presentation. Try to say something nice, such as thanking the legislator for a previous vote or offering congratulations on his or her election. Be polite. Threats and demands will only antagonize, while reasonably argued opinions will carry more weight. Come to the point quickly and concisely, using the bill number or title if you know it. If not, just be sure to state the issue clearly; many important issues will come up as amendments, so you need to be sure to communicate clearly your position on the issue itself.

State your reason for writing, what your opinion is, and why you think that way. If you are going to be directly affected or know people who will be affected by the legislation, such information can be especially helpful and significant for the Congressperson. After church people traveled to Central America with Witness for Peace or denominational mission work tours, they could speak directly about what they had seen and experienced. Such firsthand knowledge carries a lot of weight in advocacy. Offer information that can be handy for your legislator to remember and use. Cite your sources. With ten to fifteen thousand pieces of legislation introduced into Congress each year, you can help raise your legislator's awareness of an issue by effectively providing focused information.

Use your own words. If a letter is obviously mass produced or sounds like an organizational form letter, then the impact of the letter will be dramatically lessened. The legislator needs to know that you are a real person who cares about this issue. Ask questions that require specific answers. You will probably get a form letter back that is sent to everyone who writes about your concern. Use that as an opportunity to open up two-way correspondence. Write back with specific information or crisp, cogent reasoning to address points your legislator makes with which you disagree.

Then remember to say thank-you, especially when your legislator votes on behalf of your position or takes an action you request. Legislators are people, too, and they like to be thanked for what they do. So when your representative or senator casts a vote your way or takes leadership in a legislative struggle, let him or her know you noticed and are appreciative. Insults or nasty letters don't work as a means of persuasion. Furthermore, you want to maintain a relationship with your legislator that could pay dividends down the line even if he or she votes contrary to your position on a current issue—to say nothing of basic Christian decency in how we are to relate to all people.

If there is no time to write a letter, you can either send a telegram or make a phone call. Phone calls will seldom get through to the actual member of Congress. You may be able to reach an appropriate staffperson with whom you can have a more extended discussion. On some hot issues, you may only be able to leave your brief message with a receptionist who keeps a tally that is passed on to the legislator. Generally, no record is kept of the phone call's content, so don't depend on the telephone to advocate to the extent that a letter can. (Addresses and phone numbers for government offices in Washington, D.C., are listed in Appendix C.)

How to Make Effective Visits

Visits to congressional offices are another important form of advocacy. Because the legislator has many constituents and a very busy schedule, it is not always easy to get an appointment. An individual is least likely to get in, unless he or she holds an influential position in the community. A group is more likely to receive an appointment. If the member of Congress is unavailable, try to set up an appointment with the appropriate staffperson. The staffers are usually knowledgeable and capable and play a key role in gathering information that is considered by the legislator, so they can have significant influence in shaping the legislator's stand on an issue. If you had an appointment with the representative or senator and discover you will only be able to see a staffperson, don't walk out. Proceed with the same plan you had for your original appointment. If your views and lines of reasoning make an impact with the staffperson, you may end up with an ally intimately involved in the congressional office. A visit to Washington, D.C., may not be feasible, so take advantage of visiting your Congresspersons in their home offices during recess periods. You actually may end up with more time for discussion during these congressional breaks.

Before making the visit, do your homework. Gather information about the issue and the pending legislation on the issue. Gather stories about people you know who will be affected one way or the other by the legislation. Then decide who your key spokesperson will be, who will make the opening statement about your position, and what you want your legislator to do. Anticipate the issues that will be discussed, questions that he or she might raise, and questions you'll want to ask. You may want to prepare a small packet of material to leave with the legislator or staffperson.

When you make the appointment, assume you'll have fifteen minutes. Anything more should be considered a gift. Arrive on time, be polite, and dress neatly. After the introductions and informal comments, make a clear and concise statement of what your concern is. Try to include an affirmation of something positive the legislator has done recently. Be specific about the action you wish your legislator to take. Some legislators will digress, so politely return to the subject that concerns you when that happens. Take notes on what is said and any promises that are made. Offer to leave your packet of printed material and information with the legislator.

If your legislator disagrees with your information or assumptions, don't lose your temper or become argumentative. You can still convey your concerns and depth of feeling. In fact, most issues that would inspire someone to make the effort to visit Washington, D.C., are deeply felt. But if you become hostile, the legislator will probably get defensive or write you off. Discussion of deeply felt issues that remains respectful of the other person is more likely to get an effective hearing. Offer your information and personal experiences politely. If you don't have information the legislator requests, offer to get it and send it to his or her office; then be sure to follow up on that commitment as soon as you return home. Don't assume that the legislator will disagree with your position; assume that you have some information your legislator needs, whether or not he or she will vote the way you want. Even if the legislator has consistently taken an opposing position, your visit is not in vain. You are establishing a relationship and dialogue that may pay dividends down the road. More than one legislator has switched positions on an issue due to constituent pressure, new information, and historical developments.

Close with an expression of appreciation for the time the legislator has taken with you. Then follow up by sending any information you promised along with a note of appreciation for his or her time and a special thank-you if the legislator votes as you wanted. Report back as soon as possible to your group or congregation about your visit.

Coordinating Actions with Larger Networks

Politics is about power. A single individual has very little power, but when a number of individuals band together to act on a common purpose, their power is dramatically increased. For a local church involved in advocacy, your impact will be magnified if you are part of a larger network that can act in an informed and coordinated manner.

The American Baptist Churches have an office in Washington, D.C., that engages in advocacy work regarding issues on which the denomination (through its General Board) has taken a position. Many other denominations have similar offices. Newsletters are regularly produced that discuss current legislative issues and provide issue analysis, prospects for congressional action, and steps constituents can take to make a difference. Concerned congregational members should be on their mailing list.[5]

The ABC Office of Governmental Relations has established a Rapid Response Network (RRN). The RRN mobilizes American Baptists to act in a timely fashion on pending legislation. "Action Alerts" are sent to network members when an issue is coming up for a vote in Congress. Background information, legislative status,

---

[5] American Baptists may write the ABC Office of Governmental Relations, 110 Maryland Ave., NE, Washington, DC 20002. You will receive their newsletter, *Advocate,* at no charge and can also join the Rapid Response Network. Many other denominational offices are located at the same address, but check with your denominational headquarters for the correct address.

and ABC positions and theological perspectives are provided along with specific action recommendations. Through coordinated action and good timing, the advocacy impact is maximized.

When President Reagan vetoed the Civil Rights Restoration Act in 1988, Martin Massaglia, pastor of the Royersford Baptist Church in Royersford, Pennsylvania, contacted his representative, Dick Schulze, a Republican who had initially opposed the legislation. Rev. Massaglia and other church members were part of the Rapid Response Network and had frequently contacted Rep. Schulze about this civil rights bill.

> *On the day that the vote happened, I got a call from Tom Berryman, who was Dick Schulze's aide. He said, "Martin, this is Tom Berryman. In about forty-five minutes the House is going to vote, and I wanted you to be among the first to know that Dick Schulze is going to vote to override President Reagan's veto." I thought I'd misunderstood him. I stammered and stuttered and said, "Did you say he was going to vote to override?" And he said, "That's right. And I want you to also know that he has changed his mind in part because of you and your congregation's work."*
>
> *So I was newly convinced that we could make a difference. We could clearly see the fruits of our labors—and with a legislator about whom we had no hope. And I think he wanted to make the point that he is listening and that he wants to hear from us.*
> *—Martin Massaglia, Royersford, Pennsylvania*

Coalitions are also formed about religious values or specific issues so that denominations and other groups can further coordinate their legislative efforts. The Baptist Joint Committee on Public Affairs monitors and lobbies regarding religious liberty issues.[6] Many denominational offices participate in Interfaith Impact for Justice and Peace. Individuals can become members of Interfaith Impact and receive their legislative updates and issue analysis pieces.[7] Bread for the World has focused on the issue of hunger,

---

[6] The Baptist Joint Committee on Public Affairs, 200 Maryland Ave., NE, Washington, DC 20002. Their publication, *Report from the Capital,* is available for a modest subscription fee.

[7] Interfaith Impact for Justice and Peace, 110 Maryland Ave., NE, Washington, DC 20002.

including the aggravation of hunger through excessive military spending. Every year Bread for the World has an offering of letters to Congress about a specific hunger issue.[8]

Human rights are intimately bound up with peace concerns. Amnesty International is the major human rights organization, focused particularly on prisoners of conscience, torture, and the death penalty.[9] A peace group in the congregation could participate in the "Voices for Freedom" campaign, which provides quarterly information packets about human-rights abuses with religious dimensions. A variation of the advocacy action table could be set up for church members to write letters on behalf of prisoners of conscience or other victims of state-sponsored human-rights violations. Letters written to foreign government officials should be very polite, even if the abuses being raised are horrible. The purpose of the letters is to let the government know that their actions are known and being watched and perhaps to prompt the release of the prisoner or a change in policy. Venting anger in a letter may feel good to the writer, but it can put political prisoners at greater risk. The coordinated, respectful, and persistent campaigns of Amnesty International have led to freedom for many captives and the raising of the visibility of human rights on the global agenda.

---

[8] Bread for the World, 1100 Wayne Ave., Suite 1000, Silver Spring, MD 20910 (301-608-2400; fax: 301-608-2401).

[9] Amnesty International, 304 West 58th St., New York, NY 10019.

Chapter 13

Nonviolent Direct Action

One of the major forms of peacemaking is to take nonviolent direct action as a witness against evil and as a form of resistance to it. There are many forms of nonviolent direct action, from prophetic statements to silent vigils, from marches to blockades with one's own body, from boycotts to walkouts.[1] Sometimes individuals from churches engage in nonviolent direct action as members of peace or solidarity organizations. Sometimes a group within the church, particularly a peacemakers group, will participate in an action together. Depending on the issue and the degree of peace involvement in the whole congregation, general involvement of church members in a nonviolent action may be openly encouraged.

These actions are some of the most controversial steps a church can take in peacemaking. In fact, it is seldom in this country that many churches have engaged in nonviolent campaigns. One of the main exceptions was the civil rights movement, in which black churches played a central role in resistance to segregationist oppression, joined at times by church leaders from white congregations. Much of the resistance to U.S. policy in Central America in the

---

[1]See my book *Christian Peacemaking: From Heritage to Hope* (Valley Forge, Pa.: Judson Press, 1994) for a thorough examination of the biblical, historical, and contemporary practice of nonviolent direct action.

1980s was centered in the churches, with the Pledge of Resistance, a national nonviolent resistance movement, being born out of a religious leaders' retreat. However, churches that have significant participation in such forms of peacemaking tend to be small in number. Though few, the actions of these congregations are magnified by the nature and boldness of their witness.

Because of the controversial nature of these types of action, any engagement by church leaders or a congregational peace group in nonviolent direct action should be processed through appropriate decision-making channels in the church. What people do as private citizens should not be a matter of church decision; individuals need to be free to act on their own convictions. However, the formal involvement of a congregation in supporting a campaign, taking a stand on an issue, or providing training or administrative support for a nonviolent action should be handled with integrity within the normal process and accountability structures. This may take longer than some of the leading congregational activists might like, but the feeling of support and the affirmation of actions of conscience will be well worth the time spent.

Demonstrations

One of the most common forms of nonviolent action is a demonstration, often a march or a vigil. The demonstration is usually organized by a coalition of groups in the community who share a common concern. If a pastor or other church member is involved in a local issue network, she or he should be encouraged to share plans for upcoming actions with other members of the congregation. There is no substitute for getting to know leaders in the community who can work on various issues and mobilize people to respond to the issues in a timely fashion. Out of such networks the calls to action are generated.

When a demonstration is scheduled on a matter of concern to the congregation, it can be announced either publicly at the worship service or in the bulletin, or the peacemakers group within the congregation can contact people who they know are interested. Some churches will have the group from their congregation carry a banner identifying the church so that their presence is made more visible to the public. Demonstrations that may draw fringe groups seeking to increase their visibility may have heightened credibility if the more "mainstream" participants, such as church groups, are bold in making their presence known.

Christian involvement can also provide a stabilizing influence, steadying people when tensions run high. In the strike by the United Mine Workers of America against the Pittston Coal Company, the miners made an intentional and extensive effort to maintain a nonviolent protest. A local Baptist pastor and his wife, Harry and Lucille Whitaker, of the Straight Hollow Free Will Baptist Church in Dante, Virginia, became pastors on the picket lines. They led the singing, organized support, and played a major role in preventing violence when emotions reached high levels. Miners who were Sunday school teachers, deacons, and bivocational pastors were leaders in convincing other miners to abandon the use of dangerous jackrocks (welded bent nails) to block company trucks and instead hold nonviolent sit-ins across the coalfield roads.[2]

A local church can sponsor its own demonstration. The members of the Broadman Baptist Church in Cuyahoga Falls, Ohio, were appalled by a Doritos Chips commercial in which an elderly woman was run over by a steamroller while the bag of chips she was munching was rescued. In response to the blatant ageism and violence of the commercial, Pastor Jeff Scott devised a demonstration in which someone dressed as a senior citizen drove a steamroller over Frito-Lay products. Frito-Lay, the maker of Doritos, pulled the commercial, apologized, and donated twenty cases of chips to a Cuyahoga Falls charity.[3]

Sometimes community crises will demand some sort of public witness by the churches and other people of goodwill in the area. A racial murder in Boston prompted church and community leaders to call for a march of protest and community unity through the neighborhood that had been the scene of much racial tension. Blacks and whites marched together, calling for neighborhood harmony. Many of the local pastors from their pulpits invited parishioners to bear witness to the reconciliation mandate of Christ

---

[2] Kim Christman and Stan Dotson, "Beyond Jackrocks and Prayer," *The Baptist Peacemaker*, Spring 1990, 6-7.

[3] "Protest by Baptist Church Leads Frito-Lay to Apologize for Ad," *The Baptist Peacemaker*, Winter 1993, 17.

and march together as church delegations.

Participating in public witness regarding issues affecting the community gives new meaning for church members to the teaching of Jesus, "let your light shine before others" (Matthew 5:16). Faith and everyday life are seen to be interrelated. What goes on in the sanctuary and what goes on in the streets are connected, for both the sanctuary and the street are places for proclaiming and demonstrating the reign of God.

That kind of understanding of the relationship between the church and the streets drove Al Gallmon, pastor of Mt. Carmel Baptist Church in Washington, D.C., to lead weekly demonstrations in the nation's capital. He organized protests every Thursday at noon in front of the National Rifle Association building for four months to urge the passage of gun-control legislation. The killings going on in the streets of his community required a witness beyond the church building.

> *My thrust here was that the church needs to be more involved with the community in which it finds itself . . . What I wanted to do was expand our walls, to be a church without walls. The community is our church. The problems of the community are the problems of Mt. Carmel Baptist Church.*
> *—Al Gallmon, Washington, D.C.*[4]

Prophetic Witness

Nonviolent action is not just demonstrating in the streets. Speaking boldly to the powers-that-be over matters that are destructive to human life and dignity is another form of nonviolent witness. Sometimes a clear, prophetic statement needs to be made to a community from religious leaders. As people who explicitly state a concern for ethics and morality, pastors and their congregations have a responsibility to carry out the prophetic ministry of speaking truth to political leaders and to the community as a whole. Churches can have a visible impact by speaking out publicly on moral issues that affect the peace of the community.

When Arizona refused to recognize the national observance of Martin Luther King, Jr., Day, two Phoenix pastors lead the fight to

---

[4]Christie Goodman, "Profile of Rev. Al Gallmon," *Baptist Peacemaker*, Fall 1993, 11.

recognize the holiday. Warren Stewart of First Institutional Baptist Church and Paul Eppinger of First Baptist Church gave strong and visible leadership in the three-year campaign that finally led to legislation to observe the holiday. As a black man and a white man working together on the project, they modeled the "beloved community" ideal of Dr. King that they were calling the Arizona community to remember and honor.

A local church can even take its message to major world powers. When a U.S.-U.S.S.R. summit between President Reagan and Soviet President Gorbachev in 1985 was looking like a mere "getting acquainted" meeting, the members of Prescott Memorial Baptist Church in Memphis, Tennessee, sent a telegram to each leader, encouraging them in the quest to halt the arms race and offering their prayers on behalf of the negotiations. Tom Walsh, chair of the Deacon Board, said, "There are some people who think that this is political, but as Christians it is important to us to encourage peace."[5]

Civil Disobedience

Civil disobedience is a type of nonviolent direct action in which participants engage in illegal activities as a form of political protest against what they view as greater evils. People committing these acts of protest consider that they are engaged in "holy obedience" to a higher morality than that codified in a specific human law or expressed in a particular governmental policy. Such illegal activities might be holding a sit-in at a public place, blocking access to buildings or roadways or military facilities, trespassing on private property (such as entering the grounds of a weapons plant to pray), or refusing to disperse when ordered to by a police officer. This form of nonviolent action has been practiced for a long time, with many people of good conscience having been arrested and spent time in jail.

Most decisions to commit civil disobedience are made by individuals. However, most individuals making such a commitment do so within the context of a support group or affinity group. Occasionally, a decision needs to come before a church body. I was pastor

---

[5]"Prescott Memorial Adds Voice for Peace," *PeaceWork*, September 1985, 5.

of the Dorchester Temple Baptist Church in Boston during the mid-1980s and was active in the Pledge of Resistance. When an action of civil disobedience was planned, I presented my conviction that I should join in that action to the Board of Deacons. After long discussion it was decided that I was not acting on behalf of the church or in any official capacity, but that I should be fully supported to act out of my conscience. Another church member joined me in getting arrested in a major action in which people from a number of Boston area congregations participated. A dozen members from the church's peacemaking group participated in a support demonstration.

> *"The government of the richest, most powerful nation in the world is blocking, attacking, and destroying the life aspirations of our people." These words, from the Baptist Convention of Nicaragua, came to the attention of our American Baptist church in 1985. How would we respond to the voice of our brothers and sisters in Christ who were crying out for help from the wilderness of a war-ravaged land?*
>
> *After focused prayer, discussion, and reflection, our church-based peace group decided that we would join a movement of religious and secular organizations committing civil disobedience in an effort to bring national attention to the situation in Nicaragua. We hoped our collective action would change U.S. policy in the region.*
>
> *Civil disobedience? But I wasn't raised to break the law! Yet, as a community of believers, we were convinced that God would have us break a human law in order to obey God's law of justice and righteousness. Only in a community of faith, with the Word of God before us and the confirmation of the Holy Spirit, could I be committed to an action so contrary to my upbringing. Nine years later I am certain that God led us to do the right thing at the right time.*
>
> *—Katherine Vignoli, Milton, Massachusetts*

For people who affirm the importance of the individual conscience, acts of civil disobedience need to be recognized as highly committed works of conscience, whether or not one agrees with the position or the tactics of the one engaged in the action. The congregation may not endorse the action, but the members should affirm acting out of the fullness of our ethical convictions as followers of Christ. As one deacon expressed to me during the discussion of civil disobedience, "I don't agree with you, but I will stick up till the end in this church for your right to do what your conscience tells you to do." That deacon was a good church leader and a good Baptist!

Nonviolent actions, especially when people are engaged in civil disobedience, should not be taken lightly. Tensions may be high, and participants need to be well disciplined. That discipline comes through preparation and training. Experienced peace groups always provide nonviolence training prior to their actions, mandating it for those who will risk arrest. Churches can host training events or let the peace groups hold the training in the church facility. During the civil rights movement, marchers were trained in the churches prior to hitting the streets. They had to sign a "commitment card" about their physical and verbal conduct as well as their spiritual preparation.[6] During Pledge of Resistance actions, many local churches opened their doors for day-long training sessions, often with the congregational peace group as hosts and beneficiaries of the training themselves.

---

[6] The text of the "commitment card" used in the Birmingham movement is found in Martin Luther King, Jr., *Why We Can't Wait* (New York: Penguin Books, 1993), 63-64.

Chapter 14

Ministry to the Victims

One form of peacemaking is the direct ministry to the victims of violence, whether the violence takes place in the home, in the streets, or on battlefields. Wars, both intimate and international, create victims. All of us are victims to some extent; we all bear the cost of living in a violent society and world. But many people pay a disproportionate price for that violence. Besides the dead are those who are wounded and maimed, those who are psychologically scarred, those who are displaced, those who are orphaned and widowed or who have lost their children.

Sometimes aiding people who are victims of violence is an expression of Christian compassion that flows fairly easily from the heart of our faith. But at other times the victims are pawns in power games between combatants, and people who would help them get drawn into the conflict as well. Ministry to the victims can be very costly to a church that practices peacemaking by helping others with a neighborly, good-Samaritan type of love.

This chapter explores some ways that victims of violence can be served by a congregation. Some of these ways are more familiar and traditional forms of ministry. Other ways are riskier and hence not employed as frequently and are only appropriate in certain historical contexts. All draw inspiration from the teachings of Jesus:

For I was hungry and you gave me food, I was thirsty and you gave me something to drink, I was a stranger and you welcomed me, I was naked and you gave me clothing, I was sick and you took care of me, I was in prison and you visited me (Matthew 25:35-36).

As churches have cared for the victims of war and violence, they have cared for the Christ who suffers along with them.

From Charitable to Prophetic Relief Assistance

Each war or riot takes its toll of human suffering, sometimes expressed in a flood of refugees seeking safety from the shooting and bombing. A host of Christian agencies have been formed to distribute aid to refugees and other victims of large-scale violence. Each denomination has a channel for receiving funds from local churches and passing them on to ecumenical agencies or local churches involved in direct service to the victims of whatever catastrophe has occurred.[1] When a particular conflict is of concern to a congregation, a special offering can be taken to provide aid to the victims of that conflict. Posters to promote the offering can be made using a collage of newsmagazine photos and newspaper headlines. This will help tie congregants' faith actions to current events.

The end of the Cold War and the collapse of Communism in the Soviet Union brought about a different kind of crisis. In 1991 the confusion in the economy of the disintegrating Soviet Union led to a severe need for food assistance. The Leesburg Baptist Church in Virginia met Rev. Sergei Rebrov of the Moscow Baptist Church while he was visiting in the United States. They arranged with him to send a DC-10 filled with 132,000 pounds of canned goods, dried cereals, beans, and tinned meats for distribution through the Moscow Baptist Church. They contacted the Baptist World Alliance, which, through its hunger fund BWAid, was able to provide assistance for transportation costs. The arrival of the plane in Moscow

---

[1]For American Baptists, funds can be sent through the One Great Hour of Sharing (OGHS), designated for the particular area of concern. OGHS contributions can be sent to the regional offices of the American Baptist Churches. Also Baptist World Aid distributes relief assistance through various Baptist-related aid providers. Donations can be sent through BWAid, 6733 Curran St., McLean, VA 22101-3804.

on January 5, in time for Eastern Christmas, marked a special expression of solidarity between Christians of once-enemy nations during a time of great need.

Often there are conflicts for which we may take an offering to help the victims, but the policy followed by our national government may be exacerbating the situation. This happened in Central America in the 1980s, when U.S. military aid supported wars that left over a million displaced persons from Nicaragua and El Salvador. On the other side of the Atlantic, Angolan refugees fled the violence of U.S.-sponsored insurgent forces in their country. Offerings for refugee assistance can be accompanied by calls and letters to Congress and the president calling for policy changes. Similar calls can be made requesting increases in government assistance to refugee populations, such as those fleeing Rwanda and Bosnia in 1994.

Pastors for Peace, initiated by Rev. Lucius Walker from Brooklyn, New York, combines relief work and advocacy with a prophetic challenge to government policy. The first Pastors for Peace caravan took place around Christmas 1988, as nineteen trucks carrying one hundred twenty tons of food, medical supplies, and tools went from U.S. churches and synagogues to Managua. Many local churches worked to support members who drove on the caravan, finding trucks or buses to be donated and filled with supplies and raising the funds for undertaking the trip. All along the route, as the trucks converged on San Antonio, Texas, from various points across the country, the *"caravanistas"* stopped at churches to make presentations and gather more aid.

Since the initial Pastors for Peace caravan, numerous caravans of aid have been delivered to churches and relief groups in Nicaragua and El Salvador.

The Central Baptist Church Task Force on Nicaragua was looking for a new project in the winter of 1990 when I offered to drive a Pastors for Peace truck to Nicaragua. I explained that PFP was a national activist group that already had sent four truck caravans to Central America with much needed supplies—and left the trucks there for community groups to use. "Terrific!" was the response. This would be a way we could help the downtrodden. Also, since Nicaragua had been

*devastated by the U.S.-sponsored contra raiders, our truck
could be a vehicle of atonement! The task force jumped at it.
Al Robinson, its chairperson, quickly organized a church-wide
"Treasures Sale," which netted two thousand dollars for the
project. Within four months we had collected another ten
thousand dollars from various sources in the region—an ecumenical venture—and our project was firmly funded. With the
help of PFP we had soon purchased a used Mercedes twelve-
ton box truck and began filling it with such things as educational supplies, tools, fabric, flour, motor oil, and an X-ray
machine for the Baptist hospital in Managua. I had never
driven anything that big—the truck's size seemed formidable—
but driving in that summer caravan to Nicaragua was one of
the most exciting, spiritually rewarding events of my life.*
                                   —*Gordon Bennett, Paoli, Pennsylvania*

In 1993 the first caravan to Cuba violated the U.S. economic
embargo to bring aid to Cuban people suffering under the desperate
conditions caused by their isolation. Confrontations with U.S.
customs officials at the Mexican border prompted Pastors for Peace
drivers to engage in a hunger strike until all the impounded vehicles
and supplies were released. A later caravan included over seventy
vehicles and 145 tons of aid, to be distributed through the Cuban
Council of Churches.

A local congregation can participate in this activist form of relief
by contacting Pastors for Peace.[2] Find a vehicle that someone is
willing to donate, such as a used pickup truck, van, delivery truck,
or even a semi truck and trailer—or raise the funds for its purchase.
Obviously, if a large truck is donated, a competent driver will be
needed to take the vehicle to its destination. Then use the truck with
its side painted or festooned with a banner or posters as an advertising sign in front of the church to raise the goods to fill the truck.
Often donations of used materials from dental offices, medical
offices, schools, and so on can turn waste into blessing. Ask church
members to think creatively about how they might contribute
supplies for the caravan. One retiring church member donated his
optometrical equipment to outfit an office in Cuba. When U.S.

---

[2] Contact Pastors for Peace, 331 17th Ave., SE, Minneapolis, MN 55414
(612-378-0062).

professionals are updating their equipment, their old equipment is often far better than any that has been seen in many parts of the world. Tangible projects such as filling a truck can inspire greater participation and creativity than mere financial contributions to a general relief offering.

When the Baptist Peace Fellowship of North America raised funds to buy a "food bus" to assist the agricultural program of the Polytechnic University of Nicaragua, one local congregation, First Baptist of Granville, Ohio, coordinated the logistics. Two families from the church drove the bus from Ohio to Nicaragua.

Our church helped the Baptist Peace Fellowship raise money to buy the bus. It was delivered to us, sat for a week in our yard, and was driven by our drivers from church to church picking up supplies for Nicaragua. In the end we had more than the bus could hold. For a week our congregation draped everything up the walls and across the floor in the front of the sanctuary. All that was our church's vestment for worship on Sunday morning. After the sermon, while the organ played hymns, everybody took pieces to their seats and boxed them. Then we had Communion, laying hands on the heads of those driving to Nicaragua, taking bread and cup, and taking a rag. Out we went in procession to the bus. With our rags and hoses we . . . baptized it. As it drove off, we sang "Amazing Grace."
—George Williamson, Granville, Ohio

The banner that welcomed the "food bus" at the university still hangs in the sanctuary at the Granville First Baptist Church.

Refugee Resettlement

Mary and Joseph had to flee with the infant Jesus from the political violence of Herod, becoming refugees in Egypt. Today many refugees flee war, political terror, and famine. In 1994 the world refugee population had swollen to twenty million even before the record-breaking outpouring of refugees from Rwanda. Each individual and family has a story and a need. Many can never go back home. Welcoming the stranger who has fled violence is a peacemaking ministry in which the world's problems intimately enter our communities.

National and international organizations are engaged in refugee resettlement, helping process refugees coming from various refugee camps and immigrant sites. They handle the work through the U.S. Immigration and Naturalization Service (INS). But the pressing need is for sponsors for the refugee families. That is where a local congregation comes in. Several major Protestant denominations have joined together with Church World Service to resettle refugees. A church interested in participating in this ministry should contact their denominational office responsible for refugees.[3] They will have resources and counsel to help a congregation prepare for and carry out the sponsorship of incoming refugees.

First, set up a sponsorship committee. The committee members should be people who are willing to take the time to assist the refugee family in getting settled in their new land, adjusting to the culture, and moving toward self-sufficiency. In particular, the main responsibilities will be to help the breadwinner find suitable employment and provide decent and safe housing until the family can sustain themselves from their own income. Additionally, the committee can assist in signing refugees up for English classes, orienting them to shopping, using the public transit, getting a Social Security card, enrolling the children in school, and understanding the health-care system, job requirements, and paycheck deductions.

Relationships are important. New arrivals can be invited to church and may want to attend. But some refugees are from other churches or other faiths. Gracious assistance in helping them connect with their own religious community should also be offered. Sponsorship, however, is not a contract. Once their lives are somewhat stabilized, the refugees may decide to move to be closer to relatives or friends. Respecting their decisions is a part of acknowledging their dignity and worth. Though their lives have been uprooted and they may appear "slow" because they don't speak English, refugees are normal people who have their own needs and interests and ideas of how to meet them. Be open to receive and learn from them as well. The sooner the newcomers can contribute to their new community in some way, the healthier they will feel.

The First Baptist Church of Syracuse/Jamesville in New York

---

[3] For American Baptists, contact the Office of Direct Human Services, Immigration and Refugee Services, National Ministries, P.O. Box 851, Valley Forge, PA 19482 (610-768-2425; fax: 610-768-2470).

received an emergency call from another local church to cosponsor a nine-member Haitian family fleeing the chaos of Haiti following the overthrow of President Aristide. Pastor Scott Kavenagh took the request to the missions committee, and then it was presented to the church. A senior member spoke out: "If that were my family, I would want to know there is a church to let them in." The vote to become cosponsors was unanimous and met with resounding applause. Once the family arrived, the church provided housing and health care and helped set up English lessons, since none of the family members spoke English. Involvement in the lives of these refugees has been energizing to the congregation and expanded their concept of ministry.

Providing Sanctuary

The refugee who is undocumented and unrecognized as a refugee by the U.S. government requires a special form of ministry. During the 1980s a stream of people fled from the wars in Nicaragua, El Salvador, and Guatemala. Nicaraguan refugees were often granted asylum because the U.S. government was opposed to the Sandinista ruling party and was even financing the war against them. However, the United States supported the regimes in El Salvador and Guatemala, even though the military and associated death squads spread terror among the civilian population. Though the United Nations recognized those who fled as refugees, the U.S. government did not. About 98 percent of those applying for asylum were denied,[4] even though family members had been killed and those fleeing had received death threats from the death squads.

The sanctuary movement began as church people encountered some of the Salvadoran and Guatemalan refugees seeking assistance. One pastor in San Diego found a Salvadoran man hiding in the church shrubbery while a border patrol helicopter circled with a searchlight. The pastor took the man in and later gave him a ride to Los Angeles to connect with friends. Many similar encounters stirred the consciences of church folks to act in opposition to their government on behalf of people fleeing for their lives. The South Side Presbyterian Church of Tucson became the first U.S. congregation

---

[4] U.S. Immigration and Naturalization Service, as reported in "INS Claims Sucess but Others Disagree," *The Philadelphia Inquirer*, 25 June 1989, 14.

to make a public declaration of sanctuary to Central American refugees.

Drawing on the biblical image of "cities of refuge" (Numbers 35:9-15), over three hundred more churches and synagogues declared themselves "sanctuary congregations," places of refuge for those fleeing political violence. Over fifty thousand Americans of various faiths were involved in the national sanctuary movement in one form or another. Churches opened apartments in their facilities for the refugees to live in and provided speaking engagements, often with the refugee masked. They provided transportation to other sanctuary sites on a new "underground railroad" until the refugees could safely reach Canada, where they were freely welcomed.

Declaring a church a sanctuary congregation was no easy decision. The process usually involved prayerful study of both the situation in Central America and the stringent federal penalties for harboring "illegal aliens." The congregation would follow its decision-making procedures and come out with a public declaration, which would usually be sent to the local press, the INS, and the U.S. attorney general. Then a sanctuary committee would be formed to carry on the coordinating work of mobilizing the congregation to provide for the needs of the refugees and to connect with the sanctuary network. Housing, food, clothing, education, and employment needed to be arranged, as well as arrangements to receive the refugees.

Sanctuary was provided publicly not only to meet the needs of Central Americans fleeing violence; it was also a form of public education and political protest. Refugees who took sanctuary in the churches and synagogues did so with a commitment to help in publicizing the conditions from which they were fleeing, and churches hosted public events where those in sanctuary would tell their stories and experiences of repression and flight.

It was Friday afternoon of Memorial Day weekend when two or three cars from the Immigration and Naturalization Service (INS) pulled up on a street corner of our city and took Alejandro away from his wife. The Gómez family was being given sanctuary by several churches and one synagogue in our community. Over the months of their stay, they had spoken in many churches about the suffering in El Salvador, and the news of the sanctuary movement had been well publicized by the religious communities. The Gómezes were away from their home in the church on that Friday, and somehow the INS knew it and seized Alejandro.

The news of Alejandro's capture spread rapidly through the media. For several hours his wife had no idea where he was, a painful experience for a woman from El Salvador where people disappear forever. Finally we learned that he was sixty miles away and that bail was set at fifty thousand dollars cash. It was a holiday weekend; banks were closed.

The synagogue worshipers were informed at Friday night services. People dropped in off the street to one of the churches, bringing money and interest-free loans. In less than twenty-four hours, fifty thousand dollars in cash had been raised, and Alejandro was returned to his family. It was a great day!

—Dick Myers, West Henrietta, New York

Providing sanctuary was risky. Churches were vandalized, and government informants infiltrated church meetings and Bible studies. Even more serious steps were taken against churches in Arizona, where sanctuary workers—including a pastor, two priests, and a nun—were arrested and tried. Seven people were convicted, but the sanctuary movement continued. Finally the Congress passed legislation granting extended departure status to Salvadoran and Guatemalan refugees, validating the moral stand taken by the sanctuary congregations.

When we began this journey, I think we began it a little bit naïvely, not realizing the profound spiritual journey upon which we were embarking. When we received these people into our midst and began to love them and receive love from them, and these were our sisters and brothers in Christ from Central America, we began to be attached in a way we never expected before. It brought to us a sense of community, to what I can imagine the disciples must have experienced with Christ, a real sense of family, of community in Christ. This was extremely rewarding for us.

For us then we began to see we were starting to scratch the surface of what it means to take up the cross. The churches in Central America have taken up the cross, and we were just

beginning. We've experienced things like rocks through our
windows. At Christmastime we had two barbells thrown
through stained-glass windows. We've had our church graffi-
tied. We've had informants in our church. So we have felt this
in a very, very small way. We've begun to feel what it means
when you take up the gospel, and take it seriously, but I feel
we're still scratching the surface.
                    —*Barbara Heibert-Crepe, Seattle, Washington*[5]

With the ebbing of the refugee crisis in Central America, sanctuary has faded as a movement, but there continue to be situations
in which providing refuge for victims of war may be appropriate.
During the Persian Gulf crisis and war, some churches, such as
University Baptist in Seattle and Riverside Church in New York
City, declared themselves sanctuaries for conscientious objectors
refusing the call-up of the National Guard. Many Hispanic and
Haitian churches have provided assistance to illegal immigrants
who are often fleeing political violence, but they maintain a low
profile because of the vulnerability of many members in their
congregations to INS investigation. Such churches help undocumented refugees find safety, shelter, jobs, and a new beginning.
Whatever the legal status of these victims of violence, Christian
compassion compels these congregations to act on their behalf with
tangible and protective assistance.

Caring for the Victims among Us

There are victims of violence who are not far away and who have
not fled here from distant lands. These victims are in our own
congregations and neighborhoods. Some are victims of violence in
homes. Some are victims of violence in our streets and communities. Some are victims of wars who have come home but not found
peace. Peacemaking ministry needs to be extended to them as well.

Statistics about family violence suggest that there are victims of
physical and sexual abuse in every congregation as well as offend-
ers. A church can be a safe place for a victim if it is a place where

---

[5]Quoted in "Sanctuary: An Exercise in Faith," a video produced by the
Office of Communications, American Baptist Churches, 1986.

[6]An excellent introductory resource is Melissa A. Miller's *Family Violence:*
The Compassionate Church Responds (Scottdale, Pa.: Herald Press, 1994).

truth can be told, abuse acknowledged and named, and where love is available to support the journey of healing.[6] A supportive atmosphere can be fostered by giving attention to biblical stories of abuse and inviting survivors of abuse to tell their stories. This can be done in a worship service on that theme or in a Bible study or church school class. Recognize the need to tell stories and process anger and grief. Justice is a fundamental concern because the abuse occurs out of an unjust power relationship. Abuse can provide an excellent example of the difference between forgiveness and reconciliation. Community services related to domestic violence can be publicized and supported. Local shelters for battered women and families can be recipients of drives for food, furniture, and volunteers. Volunteers in shelters can be honored for their work. Support groups can be formed for victims and survivors of incest or rape or domestic violence. Riverside Baptist Church in Washington, D.C., formed a group called Survivors of Incest Anonymous, a small group for women only.

As a survivor of incestuous rape, I have found it is important to have a support system in place—a safe place—as I work through my pain, anger, guilt, and all of the unhealthy behaviors I learned as a child to survive in a dysfunctional and abusive environment.

I have found a safe haven in my church and the weekly incest support group I attend. The understanding and support of the pastor and congregation allows me to heal . . . to grow in Christ; and as a result I am able to give back to others. I organized a weekly, twelve-step support group for survivors of incest and/or rape at my church. I am committed to this ministry and to those persons who are still in pain and/or denial. I am committed to tell my story so that others will know that healing is possible through the church . . . through twelve-step support groups. I believe that only after we come to understand that a "power" greater than ourselves can restore us to sanity can we come to name who our "Higher Power" is. And for me today, I can name my "Higher Power." I call him Jesus . . . I call him Lord . . . I call him God!

It started out of my own needs. In the meetings, you are encouraged to show support. There is a lot of love shown—and a lot of healing takes place. The first night I started the group,

I was in the basement of the church with my brochures and candles lit, waiting. No one showed up. I was back the next week. Soon there were three women.
                                    —Amerah Shabazz, Washington, D.C.

The support group for survivors of rape and incest at Riverside now often has twenty women at the weekly meetings.

Five women at the First Baptist Church in Nashua, New Hampshire, came together seeking help for healing as survivors of childhood incest and rape. They sponsored a workshop to which over a hundred people came. Many were referred to counselors for help in healing, and a special service of healing and reconciliation was held at the end of the workshop. The program had such an impact that area churches and the state prison asked them to hold workshops as well.

With sexual abuse in churches exploding periodically on the front pages of newspapers, a congregation would be wise to take a thorough look at the issue and develop a policy about how to handle the various forms of abuse if they should arise, including sexual abuse or harassment by clergy. A policy can be developed that states the basic values and commitments of the church and a procedure to handle accusations, make decisions, and process feelings. Training can also be provided to teachers in the church school or in child-care programs for how to spot abuse and make appropriate interventions.[7] Even naming abuse publicly can be a major step forward. Sermons or Bible studies on the experiences of Hagar, Bathsheba, Tamar, of Jephthah sacrificing his daughter, and the Levite offering his daughter to be raped and murdered by a mob all can speak to the horror that many people, mostly women and children, endure daily (see Genesis 16 and 21, 2 Samuel 11, 2 Samuel 13, Judges 11, and Judges 19 respectively).

Support groups can be formed for other victims as well. Veterans dealing with post-traumatic stress can benefit from support groups along with others victims of violence.

I was not a loud protester of the Vietnam War but did work against it. It was more than fifteen years after the war that I

---

[7] For a brief outline of what a teacher can do, see Merry L. Rader, "Child Abuse: What Every Church School Teacher Should Know," *Baptist Leader*, June 1987, 15-16.

thought, "If you're such a peacemaker, why not make peace with the veterans?" It occurred to me that I had never welcomed the warriors home. I began attending a men's support group at the local Veterans' Outreach Center. It was an interesting mix of war veterans and war protester, and difficult for all of us. I quickly learned that some of the biggest victims of war are those who fight in it—that the enemy is not the Vietnamese, not the U.S. military, but war itself. As the veterans and I tried to hear one another, we experienced anger, self-righteousness, fear, and hurt. But slowly, over the months, we discovered that we belong together and found new respect and love for each other. I am very grateful to these men, and one woman, who are now my friends.

—Dick Myers, West Henrietta, New York

When a particular support group is not available, a Bible study or prayer group may play that role for an individual. In one church an adult church school class had developed close bonds among the members. One veteran was having trouble sleeping. As he talked with the teacher, he related an incident troubling him from his experience in the military. He later told it to the whole class with intense feeling and detail—an incident in which he had killed two people in the line of duty. Though he had done his job as a soldier well, he was still scarred by fear and revulsion over the event. The night after that class, the veteran had his first good sleep in many weeks.

When a group has grown close enough for members to risk sharing their deepest pains, the group can help with healing by listening, loving, not trying to fix, but just being present. A congregation can be taught through sermons, leadership training, and in study groups how to listen supportively to people sharing painful stories. Not just pastors but all the members of the congregation have the capacity to be friends to whom a person can turn for compassion and understanding. Deeper assistance may require a referral to the pastor or to counselors, but even with all the best therapy, a network of caring friends is still vital to the healing and recovery process.

Chapter 15

Peacemaking in the Community

Peace issues are not matters just for other countries or for Washington D.C. The need for peacemaking can be as near as the doorstep of the church. The two major causes of war in the world today are racial/ethnic prejudice and economic injustice—problems that are deeply ingrained in our whole society in the United States. Problems with racism or economic disparity at their root, or a combination of the two, create some of the most volatile conflicts in our cities, towns, and rural communities. In a country whose founding included the near extermination of one race and the enslavement of another, we are heirs of a complex mess of power relationships, stereotypes, myths, and fears that undermine the peace of our communities.

But as Christian churches we are also bearers and witnesses of the gospel of reconciliation. The Christ who has broken down the dividing wall between us has also given us the ministry of reconciliation (Ephesians 2:14-16; 2 Corinthians 5:18). The church can be a place in which we see reconciliation operate, though our track record of ethnic separation shows we are more swayed by the customs of the divided world than the power of the reconciling gospel. Our shortcomings should not make us timid in the cause of community peacemaking, however. Rather we can move ahead with a humble leadership, confessional in style. As Christians we do not have ethnic and economic issues all worked out, but we do know of God's ideal, of the vision of community where people from every tongue, tribe, and nation come together as one, and where justice flows down like a mighty river (see Revelation 7:9-10 and Amos 5:24).

Peacemaking in the local community requires integrity because the church will be seen by its neighbors over a long period of time. Taking a public stand will have some risk because the issues of local conflicts are often more intensely felt than the issues that might send us on a march to the Capitol. Our toughest peacemaking ministry, and our most strategic, is in our own hometown.

Racial and Ethnic Peacemaking

Racial and ethnic divides are a perennial problem that have taken a particularly hideous and demonic form in the twentieth century. From Hitler's slaughter of the Jews in Nazi-held territories to the tribal massacres in Rwanda, we have seen a global orgy of ethnic violence. Long memories fuel the fires in places like the former Yugoslavia, where evils committed centuries ago become the excuses for the commission of new acts of evil. The survivors of one horror become the perpetrators of another. But these evils that shock us across the globe can be found close at home, too.

Racism and ethnic prejudice have a long history in the United States. Native peoples were often thought of as "savages" and nonpersons and victimized by wars of extermination, forced relocations, and confinement to barren reservations. African peoples were enslaved, legally labeled three-fifths of a person, and even in an emancipated state were stigmatized by institutionalized racism. Immigrants have been targets for their "otherness" in successive waves: "Irish need not apply" signs, Italians tried in prejudicial hysteria, Jews excluded from civic organizations and their synagogues vandalized, Chinese hired to work in the sweatshops and lay the railroads, Japanese interred in concentration camps, Arabs firebombed to vent rage against Saddam Hussein, and on and on. No U.S. community is free of racism and its ugly, volatile spirit. If the gospel has any validity in this country and in this moment of history, it must work at the point of racial and ethnic conflict.

Many local churches are laboring hard for reconciliation in their communities. Establishing partner relationships between ethnically different congregations has been a frequent form of reconciliation ministry. (Partner relationships are fully discussed in chapter 8.) However, the motive for entering into a partner-church relationship can sometimes be misguided. Our conscience can prod us to recognize the sin in our prejudice and its most vicious manifestations. Then, out of a feeling of guilt and wanting to do what is right, a congregation can try to build a relationship with a different ethnic congregation and perhaps participate in some unity activity. The good-intentioned temptation is to look for a warm feeling of acceptance that eases the guilt but not go to the deeper levels, where the roots of conflict lie. This is particularly true of white churches. Injustice is always involved, and reconciliation that does not also include justice building is not the genuine article. Becoming a partner in establishing justice is essential for the healing of reconciliation to take place. A church that wants to be a local peacemaker will have to get involved in the sometimes murky and costly issues of justice as well.

Some basic peacemaking activities include participating in community coalitions for unity or protesting racial/ethnic violence. After a racial murder in Boston, members of many churches joined with others from the community in a march through the affected neighborhood, a type of action that has been done in many cities as an affirmation of the need for interracial harmony. When campaigns are initiated to make a communal antiracism witness, the local church can commit its pastoral leaders to participate and take an active leadership role. The church board or council can affirm the movement or coalition with a vote and public statement.

Special symbolic actions can be taken. Although these are done within the church, they also send a message to the larger community. In the midst of racial tension and violence between African Americans and Korean Americans in New York City, the predominately black Antioch Baptist Church in Queens hosted the ordination of Korean-born Dr. Chong Lee. Dr. Lee pastors the New Jerusalem Baptist Church, a Korean American congregation, which at the time had no permanent location. By hosting the ordination service, the

members of Antioch Baptist Church made a witness of reconciliation to their community that received much publicity in the volatile
setting of the time. Dr. Marvin Bentley, pastor at Antioch, said that
by ordaining Dr. Lee the congregation "was creating a bridge that
we hope is not only symbolic enough but realistic enough to
overwhelm our superficial differences."[1]

Sometimes the racial violence requires more than protests or
unity services. In the neighborhood of Dorchester Temple Baptist
Church in Boston, there was a firebombing of a three-story house
of black families on a predominately white street. The tension had
been building in the community over racial turf issues, and this
triple-decker was becoming a focal point for conflict. Neighbors set
up an around-the-clock watch on the front and back porches of the
house throughout the weekend. Church members organized to take
shifts on the watch. With extensive institutional and neighborhood
support, the situation was defused. It would have been easy to just
depend on the police to solve the crime or protect the community,
but racial violence requires a risky community-wide response.
Major figures and institutions in the community, including the
churches, need to affirm together that racial violence will not be
tolerated or overlooked.

When there is racial tension in the community, the local church
can be the meeting place for people in the community to discuss
their concerns, to talk to each other and to local officials. If the
church is connected to the ministerial and community organization
networks, the word can be passed on that the building is always
available in a time of crisis for people to meet to work on conflict
resolution. This will provide a place for the issues to be dealt with
as well as give the church a reputation of being involved in working
for the betterment of the community.

Overcoming the racial and ethnic divides need not be so dramatic. Much of institutionalized racism is masked by the mundane
matters of local government and administration. Sometimes the
urban/suburban divide, with attendant economic disparities, provides a geographic and jurisdictional barrier that supports racism.
State legislatures are often controlled by white majorities from the

---

[1] American Baptist News Service, "Korean Native Ordained in Black Baptist
Church," 30 April 1991.

suburbs and small towns that feel fear and disdain toward the urban centers. Churches concerned with racial peacemaking need to become advocates for justice in both state and metropolitan areas. The people of Central Baptist Church in Wayne, Pennsylvania, a suburb of Philadelphia, put their money where their justice convictions were. Besides participating in urban/suburban church partnership projects, the church voluntarily "taxed" itself by sending an offering to the Philadelphia Parks and Recreation Department for summer recreation projects that were being hurt by state funding cuts. By showing the connection between those living in the suburbs and those in the inner city, this congregation gave witness to God's call not just for acts of mercy but for structural justice in society.

Education events can be undertaken both for the congregation and the community at large. "Undoing Racism" seminars can be hosted. A forum can be set up with local political and police officials, community organizers, educators, and clergy to discuss neighborhood peacemaking. Study groups can be set up to deal with racism.[2] Shedrick Banks, pastor of Christ the Savior Baptist Church in Kansas City, Kansas, was concerned about the rising violence and racial separation in his community. He brought together leaders from a number of other congregations in the area to hold an "Interfaith Harmony Workshop."

The "Interfaith Harmony Workshop," held in March 1994, had some very positive results. It brought together persons from different cultures, races, religious faiths, and denominations of the same faith to explore ways to overcome the barriers that exist among the various groups. As a result of this workshop, a number of persons made commitments to establish cross-cultural and cross-racial relationships. A planning committee was formed to plan other workshops and activities for the purpose of breaking down barriers that prevent persons of different groups from building good relationships.

In October 1994 the planning committee held a second conference with workshops. This event resulted in action planning

---

[2]"Can't We All Just Get Along" is an excellent short guide for a study group on racial/ethnic peacemaking. It is produced by the Study Circle Resource Center, P.O. Box 203, Pomfret, CT 06258 (203-928-2616). The center also has a good discussion guide entitled "Racism and Race Relations."

in small groups as well as additional commitments to estab-
lish partnerships between persons of different groups for the
purpose of developing better relationships. The small group
action plans are being reviewed to determine priorities for
implementation.

—Shedrick Banks, Kansas City, Kansas

During election campaigns candidates can be invited to speak to church members and community voters on issues of overcoming racism, community safety, and unity. The church sends a message that these concerns are on our agenda and we expect our elected officials to deal constructively with them.

Celebrations can be held to lift up and revel in the diversity of the human family. Racism is undone not only by confronting the evil but by building constructive relationships that respect the uniqueness and dignity of each person and culture. Many churches are used to holding church fairs. The fairs could be turned into ethnic diversity festivals, highlighting ethnic crafts and foods and art forms. An arts festival could be organized by one congregation or by a cluster of churches, utilizing a range of indigenous art forms, including sculpture, painting, poetry, dance, and music. The Dorchester Temple Baptist Church is a multicultural congregation, and many times at Thanksgiving they hold an International Harvest Festival, with members bringing dishes from their own ethnic heritage. Unity services can bring a variety of cultures and languages into the worship experience. Even music in another language can be sung if the songs are simple and the lyrics are short. Learning a song in another language can be a way of affirming the validity of that tongue as a vehicle for God's praise.

A church that is serious about racial/ethnic peacemaking will need both a clear vision of what Martin Luther King, Jr., called "the beloved community"[3] and a strong dose of perseverance. Racism has marred life on the North American continent for over five hundred years, so a brief program, a unity project, or a religious commission will not end the problem. Reconciliation is a lifelong work, but one that goes to the core of being faithful to the gospel. The apostle Paul spent most of his ministry hammering out reconciliation

---

[3] Martin Luther King, Jr., *Strength to Love* (Philadelphia: Fortress Press, 1963), 54.

between Jews and Gentiles in the early church, seeing the ways they treated each other within the congregation as a reflection directly on the power of the death of Christ.[4] The work of racial/ethnic peacemaking—within the congregation itself and then spilling out into the surrounding community—is a central witness to the work that God is about. When people experience a bit of "the beloved community" that embraces all people, there is a sign of a hopeful future right in the home church. Dorchester Temple, with its dozen or so ethnic groups, sometimes closes its Communion services by having everyone hold hands in a vast circle around the sanctuary. As they sing "Blest Be the Tie That Binds" and can see people around the circle from every continent of the globe, they get just a taste of God's future in the midst of a racially torn city.

Overcoming Violence in the Community

Violence has been increasing in the 1980s and 1990s across the United States, in every kind of community. This is not just a concern for law enforcement; it is a profoundly spiritual issue that the churches need to address as such. That the United States has become one of the most violent societies on the earth, with staggeringly high murder rates, says something important about who we are as a society.

Overcoming violence begins not by decrying the rising tide of crime around us but by examining our values and our source of security. We can reflect on Psalm 27:1, Isaiah 31:1, and Hosea 10:13-14. The questions of who we trust and where we turn for security are key to finding a constructive way to deal with violence. The violence in the streets is just one manifestation of a systemic violence that is rooted in our history, our mythology, our foreign policy, our entertainment, our definitions of manhood (and, passively, of womanhood), and even our understanding of how God works in the world. The symptoms of the problem will not significantly abate until the disease itself is brought under control. The theological and spiritual work done in preaching and teaching will

---

[4] See the discussion in Galatians 2, in which the prejudice that drove a wedge between Jewish Christians and Gentile Christians and caused them to eat separately showed that they had not fully grasped the theological scope of what it meant to die with Christ and have Christ live in them.

help the local congregation to be a place where alternative understandings of trust, security, human worth, and nonviolence can be
built and expanded.[5]

But the antiviolence work must move to the streets if it is to have
any telling effect in society. Many congregations are courageously
leaving their sanctuaries to make their presence known in the
community. Twenty-five churches and synagogues in the Oakland
Coalition of Congregations decided to hold weekly vigils at the sites
of recent murders in their city. The vigils included songs, prayers,
Scripture readings, words of inspiration, and readings of the names
of persons killed in Oakland during the year. Signs and flyers were
made to explain to passersby what the vigils were about. After a
year of the weekly vigils, the project was shifted to monthly vigils,
with an effort to recruit a greater range of participation from other
members of the community. The coalition also organized violence-
prevention training sessions and community forums.

The Hyde Park Union Church on Chicago's South Side has been
one of the leading groups in "Vigil against Violence," a grassroots
antiviolence movement developed from churches and community
organizations.

> Among the means we employ are candlelight vigils, held on
> the first Sunday of each month, at which we gather and read
> the names of those killed on the South Side of Chicago during
> each year. We have been reading names since 1993. Last year
> we read 451 names; thus far this year we have read 353.
>
> We are trying to help one another—and our society—to
> wake up. To wake up to levels of violence that are intolerable
> yet are tolerated. To wake up to the ways violence and fear
> poison our relations, corrupt our institutions, and diminish our
> lives. To wake up to the reality that the carnage on our streets
> is not a local phenomenon but rather a product of larger social
> and economic patterns in which we are all implicated to the
> extent that we do not actively resist them.
>
> The vigils are occasions for making visible our resistance
> to these patterns of violence. They are occasions for private

---

[5] The Study Circles Resource Center's discussion guide "Violence in Our
Communities" provides a good resource for community conversation and
learning about the issue. See footnote 2 for their address.

reflection, and they provide a vehicle for building relationships among individuals and groups seeking to develop nonviolent strategies for recovering our communities from violence.

Our vigils have embraced a day-care center that was under seige, a high school where a shooting took place, a public park reclaimed from gangs. We work all day on Saturdays to restore public spaces lost to violence and decay, cleaning up vacant lots, planting gardens, creating parks. We take very locally Isaiah's calling that we are to be "repairers of the breech, restorers of the streets to dwell in."

—*Susan B. W. Johnson, Chicago, Illinois*

The campaign has a sophisticated view of violence. As one of their flyers states: "Among the powerful, there is much talk these days about violence. There is not, however, a comparable eagerness to talk about power. We condemn individual acts of violence. At the same time, we call to account the public and private institutions that contribute to the conditions of powerlessness out of which these violent acts arise."[6]

Six Philadelphia churches in high-traffic areas near their neighborhood schools have established safe corridors to protect children traveling to and from school. Led by Rev. Bill Moore of Tenth Memorial Baptist Church, the churches have organized volunteers with bright orange caps, sweatshirts, and T-shirts to visibly and peacefully secure intersections along the way and escort children through the area. They are endeavoring to provide a violence- and drug-free zone for the children. After one year of the safe corridor projects, the schools reported that attendance and academic achievement had increased due to the added feeling of safety for the children.

Members of the Dorchester Temple Baptist Church, in conjunction with Bruce Wall Ministries, have participated in Operation Urban Liberation. This project is designed to create a ten-block area around the church that is drug free, violence free, gang free, and crime free. For three nights the copastors of the church, many church members, and people from the community camped out in the Roberts Park a block from the church. They sang, prayed, and occasionally slept through the night. For three nights there was no

---

[6] "Vigil Against Violence" flyer for Sunday, 6 March 1994, vigil.

drug dealing or violence in the park. When one youth cynically said that the drug dealers would be back, Rev. Bruce Wall responded, "Then we'll come back to pray and chase them away."[7]

We won the fight with the drug dealers at Roberts Park with faith and sleeping bags. We want to serve as examples of what a church can do in and with a neighborhood.
                              —*Bruce Wall, Boston, Massachusetts*

Because so much of the violence has been tied to the prevalence of guns in the society, a number of churches have hosted gun turn-in events in cooperation with local police departments. A Washington, D.C., gun turn-in day involving fourteen churches saw more than three hundred firearms and five hundred pounds of ammunition turned in to police. When Charles Worthy, pastor of the Pennsylvania Avenue Baptist Church, heard how two women from a United Methodist Church in Ashton, Maryland, had organized a gun turn-in in their community, he mobilized other congregations in conjunction with the Washington Urban League and the police. At National Baptist Memorial Church the father of a young girl victimized by a drive-by shooting brought in a toy water pistol because it was all he could find in the house and he wanted to support the campaign. Church members advertised the gun turn-in in their bulletins and by posting notices in the neighborhood.

Local churches have taken on the ministry of teaching conflict resolution in partnership with local schools. The New York Baptist Peace Fellowship established Project HOPE, using a curriculum on conflict resolution written by Don DeMott.[8] Many local churches sponsored in-service trainings for their local schools. Members of the churches were recruited to be volunteers in the schools to help teachers and students in conflict resolution. Teachers and volunteers have been trained in many of the Rochester elementary schools as well as in school districts across New York state.

We know how to reverse the epidemic of violence that is destroying our society. Teaching children nonviolent conflict

---

[7] Peter Gelzinis, "Shepherds Sing to Take Back the Park," *Boston Sunday Herald,* 11 September 1994.

[8] *Project HOPE Curriculum* and *Conflict Resolution for the Elementary School* by Donald W. DeMott is available from the New York Baptist Peace Fellowship, 4408 East Groveland Rd., Geneseo, NY 14454.

resolution has been shown to reduce violent behavior by 75 to 80 percent when the training is begun in the earliest elementary grades and continued on through high school. But it will take a persistent, nagging voice of conscience—spelled c-h-u-r-c-h— to persuade school boards to provide training and materials, colleges to change their teacher-training requirements, administrators to adapt their curricula, and teachers to learn to use new techniques in their classrooms.

—*Don DeMott, Geneseo, New York*

Prayer and education about community violence can strengthen people's commitment to antiviolence efforts and bring people into greater unity to resist the forces tearing apart neighborhoods. The First Baptist Church of Fall River, Massachusetts, hosted an interfaith forum and service of prayer to end violence in the schools. Students, educators, community leaders, and church members discussed the root issues and prayed together for help, understanding, justice, and vision.

Hate crimes are a particular type of violence also on the rise in the United States. Whether directed at blacks, Jews, Asians, or gays and lesbians, hate crimes are not sporadic instances of violence but are encouraged by hate organizations, many of them with white supremacy dogmas, which are growing in number.[9] When a hate group organizes an event or when racist, anti-Semitic, or homophobic vandalism or violence takes place in the community, it is important that local church leaders do not try to ignore the issue. Direct confrontations can serve to promote the hate group, so positive counter-events can often prove more effective in making a clear statement of the values held by the majority in the community. Public witness in some form is vital. If people are victimized, pastors can offer pastoral care and the services of the church. If a church, synagogue, or mosque is vandalized, a public donation can be offered to help with repairs. Prayer services or unity rallies can be held involving an interfaith coalition of congregations. To counter hate crimes it is best not to wait for the crisis but to already

[9] *When Hate Groups Come to Town: A Handbook of Effective Community Responses,* published by the Center for Democratic Renewal (P.O. Box 50469, Atlanta, GA 30302-0469), is a thorough resource on hate groups, various forms of prejudice, and community activities to counter them.

have established communication and organizational ties with various ethnic churches, synagogues, and mosques in the community.

The winter of 1993-94 saw the people and congregations of Billings, Montana, respond creatively to a surge of hate crimes.[10] During Hanukkah, windows in which Jewish families displayed menorahs were smashed, and many Jewish families received threatening phone calls. In one instance, a cinder block was hurled through the bedroom window of a five-year-old boy. Police advised the Jews to take down their menorahs and put bullet-proof glass and bars in their windows, but instead churches and community groups encouraged their members to show support for the local Jewish families by hanging pictures in their windows. Copies of a picture of a menorah were put in church bulletins and printed in color in the *Billings Gazette*, and soon thousands of homes, churches, and businesses were displaying menorahs. The white supremacists smashed windows in many homes and in some churches, but the community resolve was only strengthened. Thousands more menorahs went up, and finally the vandalism stopped as the hate groups were unable to intimidate the determined citizens of Billings.

Gang Summits and the Church As Sanctuary

While violence among urban youth has been rapidly escalating, a countermovement had developed among gang members to have urban "summits" to try to stop the killing. The National Urban Peace and Justice Summit held in Kansas City in the spring of 1993[11] pulled together a number of gang peace movements from across the country with the support of religious leaders. In the year following the national summit, a number of city-wide summits were held—in Chicago, Minneapolis/St. Paul, San Francisco, Cleveland, San Antonio, and Pittsburgh.

Though the truce movement was initiated by gang leaders themselves, the involvement of community and church leaders and local congregations was crucial. Church buildings became the neutral ground where rival gangs could meet to hammer out peace agree-

---

[10] "A Nonviolent Response to Hate Crime," *Nonviolent Sanctions*, newsletter of the Albert Einstein Institution, Summer 1994, 3.

[11] See the August 1993 issue of *Sojourners* for a comprehensive report on the summit, including many interviews with summit participants.

ments and connect to community leaders who wanted to help the youth end their violence. The original summit was held at St. Mark's Church and St. Stephen Baptist Church in Kansas City. Mt. Olivet Baptist Church hosted the Minneapolis/St. Paul summit, and three churches in Pittsburgh were joint hosts of the summit in that city, including Victory Baptist, pastored by John Cook.

> *Our church was invited to become involved in the 1994 Gang Peace Summit by mothers who had been wounded by gang violence in the worst way: loss of a child. Our involvement helped us come to an understanding of peace in the way Martin Luther King, Jr., came to understand it, in that you can't separate inner peace from domestic peace or domestic peace from world peace. King realized that to be an advocate for peace south of the Mason-Dixon Line, you had to be an advocate of peace in South Vietnam. Being advocates of peace in the 'hood has made us stronger advocates for peace in the heart, home, and everywhere.*
>
> *—John Cook, Pittsburgh, Pennsylvania*

Peacemaking churches in areas with gang activity can and have been partners with the youth in the quest for peace on the streets. The gang members seemed to respect the spirituality of the churches as all of the summits have been events filled with a lot of prayer and calling on God for help.

Churches who want to participate in gang peace initiatives can take a number of roles. It is important for churches to be clear about what they can do and what role is appropriate for them to play. For those with outreach ministries to street youth involved with gangs, they can tell about the gang summits and encourage exploration of truces. Some pastors have been able to mediate conflicts because of the relationships they have built with the youth, cooling fires before shooting starts. Out of such relationships the idea of a summit can be formed and developed. A church where a pastor or lay leader has played a significant role in gang outreach could be a host site. Some communities have developed their summits out of their own networks.

---

[12] For more information about "The Things That Make for Peace," contact either the Environmental and Economic Justice Program, National Council of Churches, 475 Riverside Dr., Rm. 572, New York, NY 10115 (212-870-2385) or Sojourners, 2401 15th St., NW, Washington, DC 20009 (202-328-8842).

If there is a need for outside advice or contact with experienced summit leaders, a church can contact people in "The Things That Make for Peace," an antiviolence action network for churches.[12]

For a church hosting a summit, a few particular issues are worthy of mention. Security is a major issue, as most of the youth have weapons. Clear relationships must be set up with the police, but it is best if the security arrangements can be handled with a local group or company. For gang youth, police are the enemy, and often police use of force has triggered greater disruptions. All weapons have to be excluded from the church during a summit, including church grounds like parking lots. Metal detectors and searches are a must, not just to remove weapons but to create an atmosphere of safety which will allow the youth to move toward conflict resolution. Transportation will be needed to safely bring youth through rival gang territory to the summit site. Buses can be hired with security personnel on board.

Churches who don't have any outreach to gang youth but want to be supportive can play a very important peacemaking role, too. Many of the gang summits have created a lot of controversy because of fear or a desire to punish the youth rather than redeem them. Church leaders are often needed for advocacy. When the Pittsburgh City Council voted 4-4 on a resolution to condemn the summit, clergy organized and sent the mayor a letter of support for the summit with over seventy clergy signatures. The Minneapolis/St. Paul summit ran into police and municipal government hostility when a police officer was killed by a gang member. James Battle, pastor of Mt. Olivet Baptist Church and chair of the black clergy association, insisted on the need for the summit and committed his church to be the host. Suburban and downtown churches and peace groups can join publicly in advocacy on behalf of gang peace efforts. Politicians are unlikely to support summits because of their political vulnerability in being perceived as "coddling criminals." But church leaders who raise a moral voice in the community that says transformation is possible can provide strong support and prophetic advocacy on behalf of youth trying to find a way out of the cycle of violence. When the summit is held, those church leaders should come both to show their support and to connect with the youth directly. This can be a learning time for church folks and gang members.

Gang summits are in some ways like revivals. They are emotionally intense; they can help participants gain new insights and come to new commitments. But when they are over, the reality of the streets—racism, poverty, joblessness, and so on—sets in again. To maintain the momentum for peace, it is critical that follow-up programs connected to churches and community groups be established. Economic development projects need to be set up. The New Salem Baptist Church in Minneapolis has established Operation Resurrection, which works in housing rehabilitation, training gang youth in construction skills so they can be preparing for the job market even as they improve their community. Church members also help youth with their legal problems, since most have criminal records and parole limitations that can make it very difficult to start reconstructing their lives. Break and Build was set up with the support of the pastors of St. Stephen Baptist Church and St. Mark's Church in Kansas City to continue to address the issues identified at the national gang summit. Groups have been set up with youth, church, and appropriate community (including city government) participants to work on issues such as community peace, police brutality, and economic development. Pastors in Boston have initiated a ten-point plan that calls on churches to adopt a neighborhood gang as they work on a variety of youth ministry and antiviolence efforts.[13]

The Church and Peace at the Job Site

Conflict can erupt, sometimes with violence, between workers and management or owners. A community can be torn apart as the conflict in a major industry in town deepens and affects the livelihood and well-being of both employees' families and businesspeople who depend on them as customers. In a small town or city dominated by one company, any strike or lockout can have extremely traumatic and long-lasting effects on the community, including the local churches. The battle lines may even be drawn between people gathered at the Communion table or rail.

A peacemaking church can pursue a course of advocacy and solidarity with those perceived as suffering from injustice, or it can

[13] See "10 Point Plan to Mobilize the Churches," *Sojourners*, February/March 1994, 13.

play a mediating role. The advocate congregation takes sides, perhaps not on the particular points of a labor contract, but on the basic principles of fair pay, justice, security, and safety. During the United Mine Workers strike against the Pittston Coal Company, many church folks were actively involved. Harry and Lucille Whitaker, from the Straight Hollow Free Will Baptist Church in Dante, Virginia, were "pastors of the picket lines."[14] They encouraged the maintenance of a nonviolent discipline, brought meals, and led singing, including old gospel hymns. St. Mark's Episcopal Church in St. Paul, Virginia, owned 206 shares of Pittston stock. They sent forty-two miners and family members as their proxies to the annual meeting of Pittston's stockholders in Greenwich, Connecticut, to speak directly to the directors and stockholders about the injustices they were experiencing. Local clergy in Greenwich hosted the group and purchased a full-page ad in the *Greenwich Times* calling on Pittston to mend its ways. Some congregations have participated in supportive actions for the United Farm Workers, promoting boycotts or joining in marches or leafleting supermarkets.

> *I see supporting labor unions, whether they be coal miners on strike four years ago or cannery workers on strike this week, as at best only half of the job of Christian peace-and-justice-making. Three of our church folks work at the cannery, which produces cans for the local beer company (another story entirely!). When one of these workers comes over and talks about the company trying to take away health insurance, and when his son is physically handicapped and requires a great deal of medical attention, there's not much to do as a pastor except offer to support them in the strike in whatever way we can. To me, that's simply trying to "exalt every valley."*
>
> *The other half of Christian peace-and-justice-making is "laying low every mountain." When it comes to labor strife, this takes place in those churches where the owners and stockholders of these companies sit in the pews each week. The way I read the Bible, reconciliation between rich and poor cannot take place until the poor are "filled" and the rich are "emptied." My job as pastor of a working-class church, even*

---

[14] Kim Christman and Stan Dotson, "Beyond Jackrocks and Prayer," *Baptist Peacemaker*, Spring 1990, 6-7.

in a community hostile to unions, is easy and requires little courage. The prophetic ministry needs to be taking place in the opulent sanctuaries of power.
—Stan Dotson, Stoneville, North Carolina

The Northern Baptist Church in West Frankfort, Illinois, was distressed over the rising hostility in their community as a long coal strike and a utility company lockout eroded the local economy and put stress on most of the families in town. The contract negotiations were being handled a long way off, but the pain was being severely felt in West Frankfort.

As two prolonged and bitter labor disputes continued to drive more and more of our area's families into economic and emotional crises, our church faithfully stepped forward to organize a special service that became known as "United in Prayer." Our goal was to reach outside of our small American Baptist congregation into the homes and workplaces of our community to unite union officials, negotiators, government leaders, area clergy, and families in crisis. Together, we shared our pain and frustration and ministered to each other through words and hope and faith. But most importantly, we prayed together.

Why did our church take such a risk to step forward into an arena so charged with animosity and divisiveness? First, we were armed with the knowledge that God honors a community united in prayer. Only God could provide the wisdom, power, and grace to resolve these labor disputes in a just and equitable manner. Secondly, the community, particularly the unchurched, needs to hear the message that Jesus Christ and his church is indeed concerned about every aspect of life, including the struggles to earn a fair and honest livelihood for oneself and his or her family. To our church, these were difficult and trying times, but they were also a unique opportunity to share a part of the gospel that is too often ignored.
—Bill Lewis, West Frankfort, Illinois

The Northern Baptist Church in West Frankfort demonstrated that peace and justice are God's concerns—concerns that are as close as our own workplaces and hometowns.

Chapter 16

Communicating the Story

"If a tree falls in the forest with no one around, does it make a sound?" So goes the philosopher's question. Unless we "make a sound" by communicating our peacemaking stories clearly, others may raise serious questions about the value of our work. Genuine peacemaking often involves communities of people, and for those people to be moved to change, effective communication needs to take place.

Communication needs to be effective both within and beyond the congregation. The members of the congregation need to communicate with one another in order to pass on information, educate, and handle disagreements constructively. They also often need to communicate to the larger community. The circle of awareness about the issues of concern can be dramatically expanded by knowledgeable use of the media. The impact of your peacemaking can in some cases take a quantum leap as you get the word out beyond the confines of your congregation.

Communicating within the Congregation

To communicate effectively about the peacemaking ministries taking place within the congregation, two assumptions need to be embraced. First is a belief that the work of peacemaking is a story worthy to be told. This may not be a problem in all congregations, but in some congregations people interested in peace concerns may feel outnumbered and even marginalized by those involved in what are perceived as more traditional and basic ministries, such as evangelism, music, Christian education, and so on. If this is the case, leaders need to affirm the calling and labor of the peacemakers and give them proper place among the span of ministries in the congregation.

The second assumption can be more problematic. Peacemakers should assume that there are people interested in what they are doing besides those in the activist group. Sometimes activists become self-righteous and take upon themselves a "mantle of prophetic superiority." They may characterize those who don't show up at their events as uncommitted and uncaring or perhaps politically compromised. Such operating attitudes will prove divisive and destructive, contrary to the professed desire to find the ways of peace. If instead the peacemakers assume that more people care than show up at their sponsored events, communication will come across with a positive slant. It will be informational and invitational rather than accusatory and guilt-inducing.

Concentric circles of interest and ability are normal. The center circle is those who are deeply involved, investing their time and energy into the peace activities, attending meetings, planning actions, and standing up to speak on the issues. The next circle is those who are willing to come out for educational events or perhaps join in vigils and demonstrations. Many people, because of jobs, children, or other pressing issues in their personal lives, cannot get involved in the center of action. But they still care deeply and may do something if given the right opportunity at the right time. Communication is vital to engage them in peace activities at the times they do have available. The activist group could even make a list of such people so that, in addition to regular church communications, they can personally invite them to participate at pivotal events.

Some people simply have other interests, callings, and ministries that take most of their time. They may be unable or uninterested in attending events or actions but are open to listening, learning, and supporting your efforts with prayers and modest contributions. Communication that accepts them for who they are and accepts their own journey will help educate and sometimes pique their curiosity to investigate the issues further.

Then there are those who are opposed in varying degrees, including those who see the peacemaking work of the activists as having nothing to do with the work of Christ and as perhaps even antithetical to the gospel. Communication with them is still important, since you are all members of the same congregation. Try to be gracious and open, telling your story, inviting people to come and discover for themselves what is going on. Nobody starts as an activist, and some of us were even hostile to peacemaking at some point in our lives. Good communication is what keeps all the concentric circles of commitment and interest linked together and, in some cases, assists people to move from one circle into the next.

So which forms of communication in the church are most helpful? Obviously there are the traditional ways to communicate about church concerns: bulletins, newsletters, bulletin boards. These should be used as often as appropriate. Write short news reports of the peacemaking actions for the newsletter. If someone is involved in an upcoming event, announce it in the bulletin. If a peace group or a missions committee handles social concerns, see if you can obtain bulletin board space on which to post articles, photos, announcements, artwork, and so on. If the bulletin board is regularly changed and colorfully arranged, it will catch people's attention.

During services some congregations have announcements, prayer requests, or expressions of thanksgiving. These are opportunities to communicate peace concerns and events and to invite others to participate through their attendance at events and prayer for those engaged in the peacemaking ministry.

Telling the Story through the Media

There are two assumptions related to effectively getting the story out to the larger community outside your church. The first is that you are newsworthy. When you engage in an action on a peace concern, it is newsworthy. You may need to look at the best angle for presenting the story, which will vary depending on the nature of the media and the particular interest the news outlet has. But as a member of the community and part of a visible institution, your actions and activities are of interest.

The second assumption is that you are a help to the media when you tell them your story. Reporters usually welcome calls that suggest stories. You are not a bother or intrusion; rather you are an aid in their efforts to find good stories.

To paraphrase [F. Scott] Fitzgerald, the media are not like you and me. You don't just talk to journalists. You don't talk at all unless you're comfortable with all the possible uses they might make of your statement. If you do talk, better say it in your own sound bites and quotable quotes or they'll translate it into theirs. We took a journalist along [on a trip to Iraq] to help us not talk too much and to say what we meant in their language. I learned from him to make up my sentences as soon as I saw the pencils and microphones coming. Before I went on a people-to-people peace mission to Iraq just before the Gulf War, the press published quotes from federal officials to the effect that the proposed visit was in violation of law. It wasn't, but the quote made for an arresting heading and shifted the focus from the debate on the morality of war. But a good journalist, with a passion for making plain what is there, is a gift from God. Without a good journalist the prophet is silent and the people are blind.

—George Williamson, Granville, Ohio

A general step toward working with the media is to identify the local media outlets that may be interested in what you are doing. The print media include the daily papers (including the Sunday edition); suburban or town papers; specialty presses (minority or religious papers); and even newsletters of professional groups, unions, and alumni organizations to which church members may belong. Radio and television have news, religious programming, and talks shows. Local college stations may also be open and interested. Find out whom you should contact at the paper or station. To whom should you send a news release? Addresses and phone numbers can be obtained at the local library or in the Yellow Pages.

If your community has a local paper, cultivate relationships with some of the reporters or the religion editor. Ask how they make their decisions about whether or not to cover a story. You can sometimes write a feature article or an editorial about your concerns or actions. Think through what the human-interest side of your story is for the paper and then present that clearly and up front.

If your church is involved in a peace story—for example, a member is traveling to a war zone or you are holding a vigil against violence in your community—begin by writing a press release before the event. Use church stationery if possible and double-space the text, using simple yet interesting sentences. In the first paragraph, give the gist of the story, answering the questions *who, what, when, where,* and *why.* Reporters are swamped with papers and press releases, so your release will only be skimmed. Therefore, you must be straightforward and to the point from the very beginning. Use the second paragraph to give more details; then give your name and phone number as the contact.

Follow up with a polite phone call to see if the reporter, editor, or producer wants to pick up the story. Don't be discouraged or put off if your story is turned down. Keep trying other outlets, or ask if another reporter might be more available to do the story. Always be polite and say thank-you. You are building a relationship that is as important as the particular story with which you are immediately involved.

It's been exciting for me to come home and tell about what I have seen in places like Nicaragua. Telling the story to people who might have distorted ideas about "the enemy" is a good discipline. Sometimes we peacemakers are content to preach to the choir. So I have written several articles about peace for the op-ed page of our area newspaper. It reaches some 150,000 people. This makes me think hard about what I really saw, what I believe, and how I can write about it positively.

There are a lot of people who are hungry for the peace perspective. Many peacemakers feel alone because the loudest voices preach intimidation. They're glad to hear what I have to say. I try to state my point simply, tell what I saw, and be open about how I feel. I find that when I speak about the struggles of my own heart and tell of things that aren't regularly reported, lovers of peace learn that they aren't alone at all. One of my articles resulted in a new member for our church. Is this peacemaking or evangelism? Both!

—Richard Myers, West Henrietta, New York

Getting your story into the media takes an event that perhaps only fifty people might experience directly and brings it to the attention of tens or even hundreds of thousands of people. If you are seeking to raise awareness of an issue or change the policy of the government, opportunities to speak through the media need to be used competently.[1]

---

[1]See chapter 10 for some additional ideas and resources on relating to the media.

Chapter 17

Conflict in the Congregation

A Christian peacemaker's concern for peace may not lie only in the scope of the wide world or local community. Sometimes conflict erupts within the local church, and though Christians claim to follow the Prince of Peace, they can be very nasty toward one another in their conflicts. In fact, the topic of peace itself can be cause for war within the congregation! Some of the most vociferous attacks within a church can occur over peace issues, which can seem shocking to those who naïvely assume that followers of Jesus would be against war or killing. Even the peacemakers can be strident in their approach toward more conservative members of the congregation out of passion for the injustice and suffering they see. The mentality that prompted slaughter in the name of faith during the Crusades can rear up within a church, surprising those who are accustomed to worshiping together in unity. To use a military image, it has been said that the army of the Lord is the only army in the world that shoots its wounded. Pastoral and lay casualties of "congregational wars" attest to how poorly many churches handle conflict.

So what is a church to do with its own internal conflicts, particularly when peace is the cause of the war? Many good books and resources on conflict management and conflict resolution are available for the local church.[1] In this chapter the focus will be on those conflicts rooted particularly in disagreements regarding the place of peacemaking in Christian discipleship and in specific historical issues that peacemakers address.

Why "Peace" Starts Wars in Church

Sometimes conflict over peace concerns arises because the seriousness with which the peacemakers apply their faith challenges the complacency of those whose faith is at best a comfort for life's troubles and at worst a mere habit. Following Jesus always stirs matters up, as Jesus himself said:

> Do you think that I have come to bring peace to the earth? No, I tell you, but rather division! From now on five in one household will be divided, three against two and two against three; they will be divided: father against son and son against father, mother against daughter and daughter against mother, mother-in-law against her daughter-in-law and daughter-in-law against mother-in-law (Luke 12:51-53).

Taking Jesus seriously raises questions about our fundamental accountability to God regarding all we do. For those who would rather structure their lives around themselves or values of patriotism, American power, or wealth, the thorough-going commitment to Christ stands in sharp contrast to their loyalties. Following Jesus is a call to leave behind their old commitments and involvements and begin a new journey, even as the Galilean fishermen were called to leave their nets and follow Jesus into an unspecified future (Mark 1:16-20). The call to a deeper discipleship can prompt a defensiveness that seeks to avoid change and sidestep God's claim on our lives.

Often, however, the conflict is between people who all take Jesus seriously but have very different theological assumptions governing how they see Jesus, the Bible, and the issues at stake. Sincere people of faith with deep commitments to following God's Word

---

[1]Some of the best books on church conflict are Speed Leas and Paul Kittlaus, *Church Fights: Managing Conflict in the Local Church* (Philadelphia: Westminster Press, 1977); Speed B. Leas, *Moving Your Church Through Conflict* (Washington, D.C.: Alban Institute, 1985); Edwin H. Friedman, *Generation to Generation: Family Process in Church and Synagogue* (New York: Guilford Press, 1985); G. Douglas Lewis, *Resolving Church Conflicts: A Case Study Approach for Local Congregations* (New York: Harper & Row, 1981).

can come out on opposite sides of issues on economic justice, ordination of women, homosexuality, and participation in war. Within one's own framework for understanding the Bible and what Jesus is all about, it may seem obvious that one's own position is correct. We cannot understand how anyone who is serious about the Christian faith could see it otherwise. But the depth of the conflict and the intense feelings connected to it are the direct result of the integrity of the faith commitment of each side.

The spirit of judgmentalism can creep into both sides of the conflict. The "peace" camp may assume that those opposed to them are more committed to the United States as a nation and to its governing ideology than to the liberating gospel of Jesus. Those who oppose the involvements or positions of the peace group may accuse the peacemakers of being too worldly and not caring for lost souls or of confusing liberal or radical political philosophies with the gospel. Such demeaning judgments blind one to the integrity and genuineness of the sister or brother who disagrees. To work toward a resolution or at least a respectful understanding of one another, we must get to the point where we can at least listen with some appreciation to those on the other side.

A Basis for Dialogue

A foundational principle may need to be explicitly presented, discussed, and affirmed: the freedom of the individual conscience. This principle, which grew out of the experience of Baptists, Quakers, and other religious minority groups being persecuted in England and the American colonies, has come to stand as a major shaping value in American freedom. Those who had experienced religious persecution enshrined the rights of free speech and religion and the separation of church and state in the U.S. Bill of Rights. In noncreedal churches the freedom of the individual conscience guided by the Scriptures and enlightened by the Holy Spirit is still a foundational belief. Explicitly lifting up that principle and discussing its practical implications can move the conflict out of a context of rancor into one of practicing our historic faith.

Healthy dialogue on peace issues requires a weaving together of acceptance and challenge. We need to accept those sisters and brothers who think differently than we do. We don't need to accept their viewpoints and opinions in order to accept them as persons of faith. But at the same time we need to lovingly challenge each other to grow as disciples of Jesus, to stretch our faith and action so that we can fulfill God's calling as completely as possible. Besides, we may be surprised at what we can learn from those with whom we are in conflict if we respectfully listen to them.

A component of the process for handling conflict that builds acceptance and respect is the telling of stories. Each person has a journey through life that affects the beliefs and values he or she holds. Telling stories humanizes the opponent, and we can discover things about those we worship with that we may never have known. Ask members to talk about formative events in their lives regarding war or peace. In one church where members shared their stories, some told of their own combat experiences, which had different affects on different people. Others told of losing loved ones to violence or the fear and helplessness they felt. One story about the death of a brother stunned the people who thought they knew this person so well. When we hear the shaping experiences, particularly the pains and traumas, our compassion is drawn out. We listen to those with differing positions with greater understanding and warmth.

I was in a support group for people with loved ones involved in the Gulf War. My brother-in-law was killed in an army accident during the deployment phase. Others in the group had children in the Persian Gulf, plus two military chaplains were with us. We had a variety of positions regarding the war, from totally supporting the U.S. administration's policy to active resistance to the war. But as we shared our stories, there was a respect and understanding that formed a community in spite of our disagreements.

Shortly after the Gulf War, one pastor in our network mentioned the following experience to me in a phone conversation. He had been speaking out against the war and had become the target of antagonism from church members—one man in particular. During a personal conversation with this man, my friend discovered a very important insight. The church member's support of the Gulf War had little do to with political ideology or foreign policy analysis. Rather his support was stated something like this: "Pastor, my boy has been deployed with other troops to Saudi Arabia. There's a fair chance he will see action. He might even be killed. Declaring the war to be unjust will take away the meaning and significance of his death, should it occur. Please don't do that to me."

The pastor did not change his conviction because of this conversation. But he did learn some very important things. He was now much better equipped to speak to the issue in a way that was pastorally sensitive and informed.

—Ken Sehested, Memphis, Tennessee

Aside from the particulars of the conflict, the church can encourage healthy forms of discussion of the issues through providing a course on conflict resolution. This could include a Bible study on conflict resolution, with application made to the specific issues before the church.[2] Charles R. McCollough's *Resolving Conflict with Justice and Peace*[3] is an excellent resource for helping congregations work through their differences regarding issues so as to move forward as a church. The last part of the book is a training course for a congregation in handling conflicts related to matters of justice and peace. The course can be run for various lengths of time: from five to twenty-seven hours. Getting a group to participate for a full course would be a lot of work, but in the end you would have a significant core of people with the understanding and skills to work together to amicably resolve conflicts—which can be applied to all areas of church life.

Framing the Dialogue

Part of the discussion in the church can be identifying where the common ground lies regarding the issue at hand. What are the agreed-on values and commitments? Are there shared concerns and possible shared actions? Pacifists and those who belief in just-war ethics can often discern major areas of commonality if they take the

---

[2] Possible resources are my *Bible Study Guide on Conflict Resolution* (available from National Ministries, P.O. Box 851, Valley Forge, PA 19482) and Lynn and Juanita Buzzard and Laury Eck, R*eadiness for Reconciliation: A Biblical Guide* (available from the Christian Legal Society, 4208 Evergreen Lane, Suite 222, Annandale, VA 22003).

[3] Charles R. McCollough, *Resolving Conflict with Justice and Peace* (New York: The Pilgrim Press, 1991).

time to work together to discuss their positions and the particulars of the given issue. There may be disagreement on issues of whether military intervention is justified in a particular situation, but there may be agreement to support relief to refugees, study the history of the crisis, and open up interfaith dialogue in the community if the conflict has religious dimensions. The cause of peace may be advanced more by working on the points of common ground than trying to win a debate.

But debate can also be healthy. A church can encourage the acceptance of differences and the building of constructive dialogue by becoming a place where the issues can be respectfully discussed. A forum could be held on the controversial issue, with advocates from various perspectives presenting their positions and responding to questions and comments from the audience. Such a forum could be open to the community as well as church members. When the U.S. Congress scheduled debate on the war with Iraq, parallel local forums on the issue could have been held, with an advocacy table set up for people to expand the forum by expressing their views to their congressional delegates.

During the height of the war in Nicaragua, many missionaries were opposed to U.S. policy, which brought the issues of the war into the center of church life. The West Shore Baptist Church in Camp Hill, Pennsylvania, encouraged open, respectful dialogue in the church. They provided space in the church newsletter for two members to write pro and con editorials regarding U.S. involvement in the war. They regularly published opposing editorials on various issues, fostering an atmosphere of openness and honest discussion. Rather than being afraid of conflict, this church found constructive channels in which to express their disagreements so that members could be educated and make up their own minds.

A pastor needs to be sensitive to what the congregation needs and expects regarding preaching on issues. Many churches want their pastor to speak prophetically on timely concerns. Other churches have members who view any discussion on peace or justice issues as "political" and not "spiritual." Where the preaching may spark conflict, the pastor needs to beware of turning the opportunity to preach into a "bully pulpit." Members will resent being beat up from the pulpit. The pastor can best preach on controversial matters by taking more constructive and inviting approaches to make the conflict a positive experience for the church. The sermon can be one that poses contemporary problems, raises awareness of biblical perspectives and experiences, then raises questions of faithfulness in the current context. Stories rather than dogma offer more opportunity for those who disagree to enter into what is being said. Sermon "talk-back" groups keep the sermon from being the final word on the matter. This is harder for churches with an 11:00 A.M. worship service if people are eager to get home for lunch, but even a thirty- or forty-five-minute informal discussion with coffee and tea can provide congregants a time to respond with their concerns, questions, and comments. There is likely to be less resentment and less underground discontent if members can respond openly to the sermon and enter into discussion with the pastor and others in the church.

In Whose Name?

Church members can be very tolerant about what members do on their own outside of church. You can go on a march, get arrested, refuse to pay your war taxes, visit the "enemy," vote for whomever you want—as long as you don't link what you do with the church. Of course, it is different for pastors. Pastors will tend to be linked to their congregations in public events whether they want to be or not, particularly if they are involved in a controversial issue. Where privacy cannot be maintained, the pastor is a public figure identified with the church.

In controversial situations the question may arise concerning what the pastor can do, what a group within the church can do, what the church as a whole can do—and in whose name to do it. Given the potential divisiveness of any controversial issue (which many peace issues obviously are), it is critical for the congregation to have clear processes for deciding what can be said in the name of the church and for handling complaints regarding actions or comments made in the church's name. Lines of accountability and responsibility need to be clear. Then when the church or groups within the church speak or act publicly, there will be greater strength in what they do because of their stronger congregational base.

In a demonstration, for example, should the members of the

church carry generic signs, or should they take a banner that proclaims their church identity? Should the banner say "First Church for Peace" or "First Church Peacemakers Group," which avoids identifying the entire congregation with the action? The answer to the question might vary depending on the nature of the action. A general interreligious prayer vigil for peace might raise no concerns in the broader congregation, whereas a politically charged antiwar demonstration with civil disobedience actions might cause many members to distance themselves from the action. If there is going to be any public identification with the church, the matter should be presented for approval to the appropriate body within the congregation. Some churches may have made their involvement in peacemaking ministry so clear that those in peace-making leadership have been given the endorsement to act as they see fit. But for congregations that are just beginning their peace involvement or have been sporadic in their peace ministry, it is important to clearly spell out what is appropriate for speaking or acting in the church's name.

I experienced these issues during the Pledge of Resistance campaigns against U.S. war policies in Central America in the mid-1980s. The Dorchester Temple Baptist Church had a peacemakers group that had been active for a couple years when some members, including me, decided to engage in civil disobedience. I knew that as pastor I could not be arrested as John Q. Citizen, even if the church was not endorsing the action, and any jail time was to be taken as vacation time. I would inevitably be associated with the church, so the whole matter was taken to the board of deacons, the governing body of the church. I presented the issue and my convictions but said I would defer to the wishes of the board should they ask me not to engage in the Pledge of Resistance actions. After extensive discussion and prayer, two members of the board who were politically in disagreement with me spoke on behalf of my freedom to act upon my conscience. The board voted to give me freedom to do what I thought best. The church would not endorse the action, but neither would they restrict me as their pastor. This potential conflict was positively resolved because there was a previous relationship of love and respect, the process of account-ability was followed, convictions were presented with humility and respect, and as Baptists the church leaders affirmed the freedom of conscience.

Peacemakers need to respect the processes and leadership structure in a church as they plan programs and actions. It may seem to the more radical members of the peacemaking group that the church board or perhaps the pastor are too nervous about controversy or too timid about taking actions for peace. However, abusing agreed-on congregational decision making and accountability channels is not in the spirit of peace. If peacemakers are striving for peace and justice as their desired end, they are wise to use peaceful and just means. The Bible speaks of means being consistent with the end when it says, "The harvest of righteousness is sown in peace by those who make peace" (James 3:18, RSV). If peacemakers practice what they preach within the church, even amidst the controversy they introduce, then they are more likely to be heard, to bring people around to their position, and to be supported by a unified church.

Chapter 18

When the Nation Goes to War

There is no experience for a people quite like going to war. War is a consuming affair that seldom goes as planned and usually brings major changes in its wake. The major wars in the lifetimes of our church members—World War II, Korea, Vietnam, and the Persian Gulf—were each very different in how they were fought, their scope, and their impact on the country. The experience of local churches in relation to these wars was also very different, coloring the perceptions of members of the churches who lived through those periods. There have also been numerous smaller military interventions, such as Lebanon, the Dominican Republic, Panama, Grenada, Somalia, and so on. These episodes have not been as profound in the social and political life of the United States because of their smaller size, duration, and level of mobilization. Churches could ignore these minor wars in their programs and ministries for the most part. What wars will come in the future is anybody's guess, but a safe assumption is that the war will take its own pattern and present its own unique challenges to congregations seeking to be faithful to Christ's reconciliation mandate.

Though plans cannot be made to appropriately address a future war, some clear areas of local church ministry can be directed toward peace. It may seem that the tides of history are sweeping out of control over anything the church does, but a local congregation can play a part in God's countercurrent. Tending faithfully to its peacemaking ministry will enable a congregation to have an impact, if not to help end a war, to at least be in a position to move toward healing and reconciliation.

Processing the Issues

When a major war erupts, an intense level of emotion is generated by the nation to maintain the commitment needed to wage war. Political leaders and the media mobilize to shape public opinion even as the military mobilizes to defeat the enemy. The "fog of war" extends beyond the battlefield to the public. Truth becomes the first casualty. A country such as Vietnam, Iraq, or North Korea is largely unknown to most U.S. citizens, and enough sense of evil and threat must be linked in people's minds with this relative unknown that they will support the risks and costs borne in going to war. The unknown needs to become "the enemy" so that the violence can be justified.[1] In such a context trying to get accurate information and to engage in ethical analysis is both difficult and critically necessary.

The local congregation can play a role in processing the issues for the members and for people in the community. Sermons and Bible studies can be focused on the foundational Christian ethical values and where God is in history. The peace sermons that are so easy to preach during years of relative calm become more risky and contentious when the pastor is giving a message that questions the political leaders seeking to rally people to the cause. Yet those very questions are essential for Christian faithfulness. Congregants need to think biblically and ethically, and all their preparation is specifically for the tough times and tough choices such as face us in wartime.

Processing the issues requires a two-way street for communication. The pastor cannot just preach from the powerful perch of the pulpit. Members need an opportunity to speak together, to raise questions on all the various levels of experience and thinking. If there is no regular sermon "talk-back" forum, perhaps a special session can be set up. Pastors and teachers can use the Socratic

---

[1]For an excellent examination of the process of making an enemy for the purposes of war, see Sam Keen, *Faces of the Enemy: Reflections of the Hostile Imagination* (San Francisco: Harper & Row, 1986).

approach of asking questions, particularly the questions that tend to be swept aside in the rush of military and public mobilization. Special events can be scheduled with speakers to present one or multiple sides of the issues related to the conflict. The event can be publicized in the community so that the ethical discussion can be broadened.

> *Our church wanted something more humane and creative than war in our national encounter with Iraq, wanted to turn the hysterical war hoopla into mourning, wanted the fruits of repentance instead of the swagger of victory at the end. So we put up a sign outside. It invited the people in for activities meant to undo the war: conscientious objector counseling, support group for service peoples' families, weekly prayer vigils for peace, and weekly lectures entitled "Who Is God in Time of War?" Not many came, and no war was stopped. But everybody in town knew that something was going upstream through the down-gushing war mania. The book of Revelation calls this "the faithful witness" and "patient endurance."*
> *—George Williamson, Granville, Ohio*

Throughout the process of raising questions and discussing biblical values and the particulars of the conflict, feelings may be very intense. Members of the congregation may have opposite points of view. Those who call for peace may see support of the war as thoroughly demonic. Those who want to support the government and the military, or at least our young men and women in the armed forces, may view dissident voices as treasonous. To keep the process open and conducive to growth, church members need to affirm the primary call to follow Jesus. We may have disagreements as to how our discipleship takes shape, but if we can agree on the challenge to be faithful to Christ, then we have common ground. We also need to affirm the freedom of the individual conscience, whatever one's choice. Each person is responsible for the stand she or he takes, one way or another. We can challenge each other to reexamine our understanding of the facts, our analysis of the options, our values, and our priorities. People may need to be reminded that Christian unity is not derived from pushing aside the difficult issues but in sharing a common commitment to following God in Jesus Christ.

Praying for Peace

Praying for peace can be a trite, innocuous exercise or a challenging, prophetic act. When war is underway or looming on the horizon, congregational prayer can be an opportunity to express the anguish that must be in God's heart over such massive violence and human suffering, as well as a time to offer our own confusion, fears, and hopes at the divine mercy seat.

Many churches will pray for the government officials making decisions and the military personnel who have been mobilized, particularly for relatives of congregational members. This is appropriate, but one must beware of prayer becoming a blessing of civil religion. When praying for government officials, pray for both our government and the opposing side, that all might have the wisdom and courage to find the way to a just peace. Pray for those involved in mediation or negotiation efforts. Pray for military personnel from all sides. Our own family members are special to us, but each individual is special to God. Pray for our own insight and courage to do what is right in times that can be a rigorous test of our convictions. Give extensive content to the prayers, and remember that God is not nationalistic or partisan.

Mark Twain's "The War Prayer"[2] tells the story of a church service in which the pastor is caught up in the fervor of patriotism as the nation goes to war. He calls upon God to bless their troops in their patriotic work, to protect them from harm and help them vanquish the enemy. Then a stranger enters the sanctuary and walks to the pulpit to tell them their prayer has been heard, but that God heard what was unsaid as well as said. Their prayer included the tearing to shreds of other human beings, creating widows and orphans, and leaving the land desolate. The horrors of war were asked for in the spirit of love from a loving God. Mark Twain's caustic prayer is an important reminder to us of how our prayers can be one-sided and end up an affront to God. Calling for God's will to be done on earth as it is in heaven and to forgive our sins as we forgive those who sin against us will be far more reflective of the heart of God.

During the Persian Gulf crisis and war, the Fellowship of Recon-

---

[2] For a copy, check your local library for collections of short stories by Mark Twain (pen name for Samuel Clemens).

ciliation distributed an interfaith prayer that is an excellent model of a peace prayer embracing the breadth of people involved in the conflict:

> O God, you fill the universe with light and love.
> In you we live and move and have our being.
> We pray for Saddam Hussein and George Bush.
> Enlighten their minds, and fill their hearts with the power
> of your creative love.
> Guide their actions so that all civilians and soldiers in
> the Gulf area are protected from the sufferings of war.
> Inspire their decisions so that the crisis in the Middle East
> is resolved peacefully, and all peoples of the world
> learn to walk in the ways of justice, love, and peace.
> Amen.

During the build-up phase of the crisis and throughout the fighting, the Baptist Peace Fellowship of North America called on churches to engage in weekly prayer and fasting for peace. Over fifteen hundred people signed a pledge to pray daily and fast weekly. One church in New York held a twenty-four-hour vigil in partnership with other local churches, and many congregations had special prayer services, sometimes in partnership with other congregations in their communities.

Loving Our Enemies

One of Jesus' most explicit commands is also the most difficult to seriously follow during wartime: "Love your enemies" (Matthew 5:44). War runs on hatred like a car runs on gasoline. In order to justify killing not just soldiers but also civilians, they must be dehumanized in some way—a task taken on by political rhetoric, media portrayals, cartoon caricatures, and even religious condemnation. A faithful church during a war has the unpleasant but spiritually critical task of reminding people by word and example of Christ's imperative to love the enemy.

Part of loving is trying to understand. What are the valid interests of the enemy? Are those interests being appropriately addressed in any of the actions or proposals of our own country? What kind of fears does the other side have of us? Are our actions building bridges of trust or deepening the distrust?

During these crisis moments, understanding the enemy can be helped by inviting special speakers to make presentations. During the Gulf War a number of churches contacted Muslim and Jewish leaders in their communities to talk and develop joint programs to build more understanding. Though the war was going on halfway across the globe, our neighbors could help us remove our ignorance and prejudice, upon which much of our hatred of the enemy depends. Christians have a history of animosity and misrepresentation of Muslim cultures and faith, which has been an issue in the conflicts in the Middle East that continually enter our news. Through guest speakers or classes about different faiths and cultures, people who are different can become less alien and more understandable.[3]

Praying specifically and positively for our enemies is important not just for our enemies but for the spiritual survival of our own hearts in the midst of surrounding bitterness and hatred. The natural human tendency in times of war is to pray the condemnations of the Psalms: "O that you would kill the wicked, O God!" (Psalm 139:19). Jesus' prayer from the cross provides a different model: "Father, forgive them; for they do not know what they are doing" (Luke 23:34). Prayers for enemies can include petitions that their needs will be met and their fears assuaged and that they might participate in finding the path to a just peace. But the most important fruit of such prayer may be the change in our own hearts. Jim Wallis has said, "Fervent prayer for our enemies is a great obstacle to war and the feelings that lead to it."[4] My own perspective is changed as prayer draws me into God's perspective. The apostle Paul reflects our transformed understanding of others as he explores the impact of the reconciliation ministry of Christ that is passed on to Christians: "From now on, therefore, we regard no one from a human point of view" (2 Corinthians 5:16). A church praying for a nation's

---

[3]Two books on the Middle East and Islam for church use are Charles Kimball, *Striving Together: A Way Forward in Christian-Muslim Relations* (Maryknoll, N.Y.: Orbis Books, 1991) and Charles Kimball, *Angle of Vision: Christian and the Middle East* (New York: Friendship Press, 1992).

[4]Jim Wallis, "The Work of Prayer," *Waging Peace: A Handbook for the Struggle to Abolish Nuclear Weapons*, ed. Jim Wallis (New York: Harper & Row, 1982), 196.

enemies is likely to resist the hysteria of hatred stirred up by political leaders and the media.

Support in a Time of Need

War is a high-stress experience for those involved both directly or indirectly, sometimes leading to lifelong physical or psychological scars. Profound changes can take place in people, shaping new values and commitments. Pastoral care and support from a loving church family are vital for Christ's healing power to be mediated to those hurting from their experiences with war.

For a peacemaking church, providing support for members or children of members in the military can be a complicated issue. There may be strong opposition to the war, and yet those in the military are probably committed to doing their jobs well, which translates into efficient killing and devastation. It is important for a peacemaking church not to let its political and moral criticism of the war blind it to the humanity and needs of those engaged in it or of their family members. Honest disagreement can be stated within an affirmation of love and personal support. Keep channels of communication open, and let people know you care.

The church can list the names of military personnel in the bulletin and pray for them as members of the church family with special needs. Letters can be sent. During the Gulf War, a peace group in one church sent letters to members in the military stationed in Saudi Arabia, expressing their concern and prayers even though they opposed U.S. policy in the region. Following their return from war, the church can provide small group settings for the veterans to share and process their experiences, either among themselves or with some other supportive group.

Young people who sign up with the military are seldom set in their convictions and values. The experiences of life can cause dramatic reassessments of what they believe. The sudden challenge of a war situation can force serious soul-searching, which in some cases may lead to someone in the military becoming a conscientious objector or to a belief that the current war is unjust. There is little support for such individuals but often a lot of hostility, from the military and even society in general. Pastoral support to think through the issues and make a choice based on one's conscience can be a welcome and appreciated ministry. A pastor can let church members know he or she is available to work through questions of conscience with openness and understanding.

Moral reevaluation of one's commitments doesn't happen just to the young. People who have seen much of life and who have grappled with deep questions of faith and conscience can come to life-changing decisions as part of their own spiritual growth or encounter with new experiences. Chaplain César Maurás was an army reserve chaplain who volunteered to go to Saudi Arabia as part of Operation Desert Shield. When he heard more about the roots of the conflict, learned about the repressive governments of Kuwait and Saudi Arabia, and saw U.S. military preparations for offensive action, he knew he was at a personal moral crossroads.

> *I was not a pacifist, at least not then—I'm not sure what I am now. But it didn't take me too long to realize what a mistake this was. I knew that if I stayed, I would have to renounce my ministry. It would be impossible for me to ever again preach about God's love after participating in this war.*
>
> *Sometimes I still can't explain my actions, like when someone asks me, "What good was it that you chose to come home?" I can't immediately say what good it was . . . what good it accomplished. But I know I am happy with my decision.*
> *—César Maurás, Caguas, Puerto Rico*

Eventually he sacrificed his commission, an upcoming promotion, and lucrative retirement benefits to follow his conscience. He received support from his denomination and a few close friends from his home church, but most of his experience was characterized by loneliness due to his isolation in Saudi Arabia and the hostility of many of his commanding officers, including chaplains, to his refusal to support the move from defensive to offensive warfare.

Families of military personnel go through the anxiety of knowing their loved ones are in a danger zone and being too far away to help or expresses their caring directly. In the Gulf War many families of reservists and national guard members faced the additional traumas of financial dislocation because of the call-up. These high-stress experiences can be aided by extra pastoral care, special support groups, specific prayer, and sometimes by congregational financial assistance.

In some cases, the more radical peace activists might engage in civil disobedience, which can lead to time in jail with attendant family stress. Fines or lost job time might create financial hardship for the activists and their families. These church members, too, need to be embraced by the congregation with support and care.

Prophetic Voices

During war many voices are raised in support of mobilization. Voices that raise questions or protest during the deliberation stage are expected by the majority in power to join in supporting the effort once the troops are in harm's way. But prophetic voices are always needed to speak truth to the people of God and to society at large. The story in 1 Kings 22 about Ahab and Jehoshaphat going to war illustrates both the need for and the lonely calling of the prophet. Four hundred prophets raised their voices in support of the kings' war program. Only one, Micaiah, spoke in dissent, proclaiming that the war would lead to disaster. He also paid a price for his dissent, as Ahab ordered him imprisoned until his return. Prophetic voices who speak hard words are not appreciated.

Where will a voice of moral authority come from if not from the church? Harry Emerson Fosdick's great hymn prays, "Grant us wisdom, grant us courage, for the living of these days . . . Save us from weak resignation To the evils we deplore . . ."[5] During a war local congregations need courage and wisdom to be prophetic. If they fail to stand on ethical grounds when the cost is high, then the church is morally and religiously compromised.

One way a prophetic voice can be raised is to encourage advocacy by the church members. Following a service or a special event dealing with the war, tables can be set up with materials and instructions for writing Congress and the president. (See chapter 11 for details.) Often denominations will make a resolution about the crisis. A congregation can quote the resolution in a letter to government officials if the church board or membership votes to take a united stand. Local use of denominational resolutions gives special strength to statements that can all too often be passed off otherwise. When a church says that the statement expresses its position, then this voice from the grassroots adds dramatically to what an elected

---

[5]Harry Emerson Fosdick, "God of Grace and God of Glory," 1930.

politician will hear. A letter can be made an open letter and sent to publications and newspapers as well as to the individual directly addressed. That allows the prophetic word to be heard by a larger audience, making the matter a public affair.

Members of the Central Baptist Church in Wayne, Pennsylvania, felt that the peace movement and churches were being too passive or slow in their response to the developments in the Persian Gulf in late 1990 and into January 1991. When the war erupted, they promoted a "Deadline for Peace," reflecting the earlier deadline set by President Bush for Iraq to withdraw from Kuwait. When the cease-fire came earlier than the deadline due to the rapid coalition victory, the church changed the "Deadline for Peace" to an "Agenda for Peace." Their eight-point call for action included matters such as an international peace conference on the Middle East, mediation on the Israeli-Palestinian and Iraqi-Kuwaiti issues, and the removal of all foreign troops, to be replaced by United Nations' forces if necessary. The church used the deadline and agenda as an advocacy project, contacting political officials. They also lobbied religious and peace organizations to embrace the project and take it to a larger constituency. The church members were not content to just watch the news; they entered into the public discussion to try to help shape the issues.

During the Gulf War some churches, including Riverside Church in New York City and University Baptist in Seattle, declared themselves sanctuary churches for conscientious objectors. These public declarations were more prophetic than pragmatic, for they highlighted both the moral issues and the harassment of people making decisions of conscience against the prevailing policy.

Postscript

A Word of Encouragement

At the end of the 1980s a newsmagazine had a cover headline, "Is Peace Breaking Out?" My colleagues joked that my job as director of the Peace Program might become anachronistic. Not long after that, the Persian Gulf crisis erupted, then Somalia, then former Yugoslavia, then Rwanda, then . . .

The peacemaking ministry of the local church will never become unnecessary. Jesus said, "You will hear of wars and rumors of wars" (Matthew 24:6). He didn't say this to relieve the disciples of their responsibility to be peacemakers. The peacemakers will still be called children of God, but they also need to be realistically aware that humanity will always know conflict in this age.

How sweet are those moments of breakthrough when enemies embrace with tears of old sorrow and new hope! Whether we are reconciled to a spouse, a child, a parent, a faction in the church, an ethnic group in the community, or a nation with which we were at war, we feel exhilaration, relief, and hope. The valley of tears somehow seems bearable when we break out on the crest of the ridge to see clearly the landscape around us.

But then we seem forced back into the valley again. Another war erupts from a place we can't find on the map. Another racial killing occurs in our community. Another church fight breaks out over something that seems so petty. We put out one fire in our lives only to have another ignite just beyond our reach.

Sometimes we just get tired of pressing on, of dealing with *that* issue yet again, of trying to stand against the tide of our world's greed and power lust. The apostle Paul had a word of encouragement for times like these: "So let us not grow weary in doing what is right, for we will reap at harvest-time, if we do not give up" (Galatians 6:9).

When the bones and the heart ache, we need to draw strength from our faith to persevere. God's harvesttime, the future of *shalom,* will dawn. Christ has risen from the dead as the first fruit of the grand harvest of history or, to use a more contemporary metaphor, as the sneak preview of God's future. So we don't give up. We admit we can't do everything, but we also know we can do something. So we do the tasks God sets before us as best we can. However, as we labor for justice and peace in the name of Christ, it is not all struggle. We so often are surprised by the delightful breakthroughs of the Spirit's joy and of resurrection power. Peace is not just our dream, but in ways that confound the world it can be our inner resting place. Peace is the gift we find in a community of others who share our journey of faith and ministry.

War's last word is death, but war does not have the last word. That last word belongs to the living God, who says, "See, I am making all things new" (Revelation 21:5). Even death will be overcome in God's triumphant newness. The faithful peacemaking church lives—and is a signpost for that future.

Appendix A

Peace Hymns in Hymnbooks

Hymns with peace themes are found in a number of frequently used hymnals. Below is a list of hymn titles that includes the hymnals in which they are found and their hymn numbers.

Abbreviation Code

CW—*Hymnbook for Christian Worship* (Judson Press/Bethany Press, 1970)

FG—*Hymns for the Family of God* (Paragon Associates, 1976)

LC—*Hymns for the Living Church* (Hope Publishing, 1970)

NB—*The New National Baptist Hymnal* (National Baptist Publishing Board, 1977)

PH—*Pilgrim Hymnal* (Pilgrim Press, 1958)

SS—*Hymns, Psalms and Spiritual Songs* (Westminster/John Knox, 1990)

UM—*United Methodist Hymnal* (United Methodist Publishing House, 1989)

WC—*The Worshiping Church* (Hope Publishing, 1990)

WM—*Worship His Majesty* (Gaither Music Co., 1987)

A Song of Peace (FG-682)

All Glory Be to God on High (CW-58; SS-133; PH-2)

All Who Love and Serve Your City (SS-413; UM-433; WC-430)

Arise, O Youth of God (NB-446)

Behold a Broken World (UM-426)

Canto de Esperanza (Song of Hope) (SS-432)

Christ for the World (NB-37)

Christ for the World We Sing (FG-686; UM-568; WM-669)

Christ Is the World's Light (UM-188)

Christ Is the World's True Light (PH-198)

Comfort, Comfort You My People (SS-3; WC-132)

Creating God, Your Fingers Trace (SS-134; UM-109)

Creator of Earth and Skies (UM-450)

Crown Him with Many Crowns (SS-151; UM-327)

Cuando el Pobre (When a Poor One) (SS-407; UM-434)

Dona Nobis Pacem (UM-376)

Father Eternal, Ruler of Creation (CW-265; LC-516; PH-445)

For the Beauty of the Earth (CW-7; FG-1; PH-66; SS-473; UM-92; WM-76)

For the Healing of the Nations (UM-428)

God of Grace and God of Glory (CW-245; PH-366; SS-420; UM-577)

God in His Love for Us (WC-385)

God the Omnipotent! (CW-33; LC-527; PH-446; WC-427)

Heralds of Christ (LC-488; UM-567)

He's My Everything (NB-36)

Hope of the World (CW-236; LC-515; PH-398; SS-360; UM-178; WC-434)

I Bind My Heart This Tide (CW-219)

In Christ There Is No East or West (CW-269; FG-685; LC-513; NB-360; PH-414,415; SS-439,440; UM-548; WC-695,697; WM-671)

It Came Upon the Midnight Clear (CW-119; LC-104; NB-60; PH 129; SS-38; UM-218; WM-134)

Joyful, Joyful We Adore Thee (CW-1; FG-377; LC-25; NB-6; PH-8; SS-464; UM-89; WC-20; WM-36)

Lead On, O King Eternal (CW-246; FG-595; LC-457; NB-397; PH-375; SS-447,448; UM-580; WC-747; WM-599)

Let There Be Light (UM-440)

Let There Be Light, Lord God of Hosts (CW-331; PH-449)

Let There Be Peace on Earth (FG-681; UM-431)

Lift Every Voice and Sing (NB-477; UM-519)

Lord Christ, When First Thou Cam'st (PH-325)

Lord Christ, When First You Came to Earth (SS-7)

Lord, Make Us Servants of Your Peace (SS-374)

Lord, Whose Love through Humble Service (CW-145; LC-512; SS-427; UM-581; WC-426)

New Songs of Celebration Render (SS-218)

O Brother Man, Fold to Thy Heart (CW-264; PH-410)

O Day of God, Draw Nigh (CW-266; PH-444; SS-452; UM-730)

O Day of Peace (SS-450; UM-729)

O For a World (SS-386)

O God of Every Nation (SS-289; UM-435; WC-422)

O God of Love, O God of Peace (SS-295)

O God, Our Help in Ages Past (CW-23; FG-370; LC-48; NB-19; UM-117; WC-78; WM-335)

O How Blest Are the Poor in Spirit (WC-603)

Peace in Our Time, O Lord (LC-519)

Reach Out and Touch (NB-418)

Ring Out the Old, Ring in the New (NB-482)

Send Down Thy Truth, O God (PH-237)

The Savior's Wondrous Love (CW-267)

This Is My Song (UM-437)

Thou God of All, Whose Spirit Moves (PH-419)

Today We All Are Called to Be Disciples (SS-434)

We Shall Overcome (NB-372; UM-533)

We Utter Our Cry (UM-439)

Weary of All Trumpeting (UM-442)

We've a Story to Tell to the Nations (FG-659; LC-483; NB-409; UM-569; WC-733; WM-673)

When Will People Cease Their Fighting (SS-401)

Where Cross the Crowded Ways of Life (CW-268; FG-665; LC-514; SS-408; UM-427; WC-433)

Wonderful Peace (NB-296)

Appendix B

Peace Organizations

The following organizations are either denominational peace offices, peace fellowships, or religious peace groups. Where it is not clear from the title what the group is, an additional descriptive comment is included. Most of these groups have newsletters or magazines about their work.

American Baptist Peace Program
National Ministries
P.O. Box 851
Valley Forge, PA 19482-0851
610-768-2451

American Friends Service Committee
1501 Cherry St.
Philadelphia, PA 19102
215-241-7000

Baptist Peace Fellowship of North America
499 S. Patterson
Memphis, TN 38111
901-324-7675

Bread for the World
1100 Wayne Ave., Suite 1000
Silver Spring, MD 20910

301-608-2400

(A hunger advocacy network which often deals with peace concerns related to hunger)

Christian Peacemaker Teams
P.O. Box 6508
Chicago, IL 60608
312-455-1199

(A nonviolent action and intervention ministry of Mennonites and Brethren)

Church of the Brethren General Board
Office of Denominational Peace Witness
1451 Dundee Ave.
Elgin, IL 60120
1-800-323-8039

Churches for Middle East Peace
110 Maryland Ave., NE, Suite 108
Washington, DC 20002
202-546-8425

Clergy and Laity Concerned
340 Mead Rd.
Decatur, GA 30030
404-377-1983

Evangelicals for Social Action
10 Lancaster Ave.
Wynnewood, PA 19096
215-645-9390

The Fellowship of Reconciliation
P.O. Box 271
Nyack, NY 10960
914-358-4601
(An interfaith pacifist organization)

Institute for Peace and Justice
4144 Lindell Blvd., #124
St. Louis, MO 63108
314-533-4445
(An interfaith network that includes Parenting for Peace and Justice)

Interreligious Foundation for Community Organization
402 W. 145th St.
New York, NY 10031
212-926-5757
(Church and community agency for justice projects, including Pastors for Peace—see below)

Lutheran Peace Fellowship
1710 11th Ave.
Seattle, WA 98122

Mennonite Central Committee
21 S. 12th St., Box M
Akron, PA 17501
717-859-1151

New Call to Peacemaking
P.O. Box 500
Akron, PA 17501
717-859-1958
(Grassroots peace fellowship for the historic peace churches)

Pastors for Peace
331 17th Ave., SE
Minneapolis, MN 55414
612-378-0062
(Project of IFCO—see above—to take aid caravans to Central America and the Caribbean)

Peace with Justice Program
General Board of Church and Society of the United Methodist
    Church
100 Maryland Ave., NE
Washington, DC 20002
202-488-5600

Presbyterian Peacemaking Program
100 Witherspoon St.
Louisville, KY 40202-1396
502-569-5784

Sojourners
2401 15th St., NW
Washington, DC 20078
202-328-8757

(Christian community with various peace ministries, including publishing *Sojourners* magazine)

U.S. Interreligious Committee for Peace in the Middle East
Greene & Westview, 3rd Floor
Philadelphia, PA 19119
215-438-4142

Witness for Peace
2201 P St., NW, Rm. 109
Washington, DC 20037
202-797-1160

(Interfaith nonviolent intervention and witness project in Central America)

Appendix C

Advocacy Addresses

The following addresses and salutations are for use in letters of advocacy related to political issues:

President
The President
The White House
Washington, DC 20500
Dear Mr. President:

Senators
The Honorable _____
United States Senate
Washington, DC 20510
Dear Senator _____:

Representatives
The Honorable _____
U.S. House of Representatives
Washington, DC 20515
Dear Mr./Ms. _____:

Judiciary
The Honorable _____
Associate Justice (or Chief Justice, as appropriate)
United States Supreme Court

Washington, DC 20543
My dear Justice (or Chief Justice)_____:

Members of the Cabinet
The Honorable _____
Department of _____
Washington, DC (ZIP)
Dear Secretary _____:

Zip Codes:
Agriculture—20250
Attorney General—20530
Commerce—20230
Defense—20301
Education—20202
Energy—20585
Health and Human Services—20201
Housing and Urban Development—20410
Interior—20240
Labor—20210
State—20520
Transportation—20590
Treasury—20220
Veterans Affairs—20420

United Nations Ambassador
Ambassador_____
United States Mission to the United Nations
799 United Nations Plaza
New York, NY 10017
Dear Ambassador _____:

Phone Numbers in Washington:
Capitol (Call this number for all House and Senate offices):
202-224-3121
White House:
202-456-1414 (Switchboard)
202-456-1111 (Comment Line)
Supreme Court:
202-479-3000 (General Information)

Appendix D

Bibliography

Bainton, Roland. *Christian Attitudes Toward War and Peace*. Nashville: Abingdon Press, 1960.

Barrett, Lois. *The Way God Fights: War and Peace in the Old Testament*. Scottdale, Pa.: Herald Press, 1987.

Bobo, Kimberly. *Lives Matter: A Handbook for Christian Organizing*. Kansas City, Mo.: Sheed and Ward, 1986.

Branding, Ronice E. *Peacemaking: The Journey from Fear to Love*. St. Louis: CBP Press, 1987.

Brown, Robert McAfee. *Unexpected News: Reading the Bible with Third World Eyes*. Philadelphia: Westminster, 1984.

Bruland, Esther Byle, and Mott, Stephen Charles. *A Passion for Jesus; A Passion for Justice*. Valley Forge, Pa.: Judson Press, 1983.

Buttry, Daniel L. *A Bible Study Guide on Conflict Resolution*. Valley Forge, Pa.: National Ministries (ABC/USA), 1994.

Buttry, Daniel L. *A Bible Study Guide: War and Peace*. Valley Forge, Pa.: National Ministries (ABC/USA), 1990.

Buttry, Daniel L. *Christian Peacemaking: From Heritage to Hope*. Valley Forge, Pa.: Judson Press, 1994.

Clouse, Robert G., ed. *War: Four Christian Views*. Downers Grove, Ill.: InterVarsity Press, 1981.

Dekar, Paul R. *For the Healing of the Nations: Baptist Peacemakers*. Macon, Ga.: Smyth & Helwys Publishing, 1993.

Elmer, Duane. *Cross-Cultural Conflict: Building Relationships for Effective Ministry*. Downers Grove, Ill.: InterVarsity Press, 1993.

Herzog, William R., II. *Parables as Subversive Speech: Jesus as Pedagogue of the Oppressed*. Louisville, Ky.: Westminster/John Knox Press, 1994.

Huber, Jane Parker, ed. *Peacemaking Through Worship, Volume II*. Louisville, Ky.: Presbyterian Peacemaking Program.

McCollough, Charles R. *Resolving Conflict with Justice and Peace*. New York: Pilgrim Press, 1991.

McGinnis, James. *Journey into Compassion: A Spirituality for the Long Haul*. Maryknoll, N.Y.: Orbis, 1989.

McSorely, Richard. *New Testament Basis of Peacemaking*. Scottdale, Pa.: Herald Press, 1979.

Mennonite Conciliation Service. *Mediation Training Manual: Skills for Constructive Conflict Transformation*. Akron, Pa.: Mennonite Conciliation Service, 1992.

Mock, Ron, ed. *The Role Play Book: Thirty-two Hypothetical Situations for the Practice of Interpersonal Peacemaking Skills*. Akron, Pa.: Mennonite Conciliation Service, 1988.

O'Gorman, Angie, ed. *The Universe Bends Toward Justice: A Reader on Christian Nonviolence in the U.S.* Philadelphia: New Society Publishers, 1990.

Pipkin, H. Wayne, ed. *Seek Peace and Pursue It: Proceedings from the 1988 International Baptist Peace Conference*. Memphis, Tenn.: Baptist Peace Fellowship of North America, 1989.

Presbyterian Peacemaking Program. *Peacemaking Through Worship*. Louisville, Ky.: Presbyterian Peacemaking Program.

Rocky Mountain Peace Center. *Communities of Conversation and Action: A Manual for Building Community*. Boulder, Colo.: Rocky Mountain Peace Center, 1988.

Rogers, Ingrid. *Swords into Plowshares: A Collection of Plays About Peace and Social Justice*. Elgin, Ill.: Brethren Press, 1983.

Sehested, Ken, ed. *Dreaming God's Dream: Study Materials for Church, Home and School: Learning-Based Activities for Six Age Groups*. Memphis, Tenn.: Baptist Peace Fellowship of North America, 1989.

Sider, Ronald J. *Christ and Violence*. Scottdale, Pa.: Herald Press, 1979.

Sider, Ronald J. *Nonviolence: The Invincible Weapon?* Dallas: Word Publishing, 1989.

Stassen, Glen. *Journey into Peacemaking*. Memphis, Tenn.: Brotherhood Commission, Southern Baptist Convention, 1983.

Stassen, Glen. *Just Peacemaking: Transforming Initiatives for Justice and Peace*. Louisville, Ky.: Westminster/John Knox Press, 1992.

Taylor, Richard K. *Peace and Justice Ministry: A Practical Guide*. Dubuque, Iowa: Brown-Roa, 1994.

Villa-Vicencio, Charles, ed. *Theology and Violence: The South Africa Debate*. Grand Rapids, Mich.: Wm. B. Eerdmans, 1987.

Washburn, Patricia, and Gribbon, Robert. *Peacemaking Without Division: Moving Beyond Congregational Apathy and Anger*. Washington, D.C.: The Alban Institute, 1986.

Wink, Walter. *Violence and Nonviolence in South Africa: Jesus' Third Way*. Philadelphia: New Society Publishers, 1987.

Winn, Albert Curry. *Ain't Gonna Study War No More: Biblical Ambiguity and the Abolition of War*. Louisville, Ky.: Westminster/John Knox Press, 1993.

Wollman, Neil, ed. *Working for Peace: A Handbook of Practical Psychology and Other Tools*. San Luis Obispo, Calif.: Impact Publishers, 1985.

Appendix E

Children's Bibliography

For Parents, Youth Workers, and Teachers

Campolo, Tony. *Ideas for Social Action: A Handbook on Mission and Service for Christian Young People*. Grand Rapids, Mich.: Zondervan Publishing House, 1983.

Carlsson-Paige, Nancy, and Levin, Diane E. *Who's Calling the Shots? How to Respond Effectively to Children's Fascination with War Play and War Toys*. Philadelphia: New Society Publishers, 1990.

Condon, Camy, and McGinnis, James. *Helping Kids Care: Harmony-Building Activities for Home, Church and School*. Bloomington, Ind.: Meyer-Stone Books, 1988.

Crary, Elizabeth. *Children's Problem-Solving Series*. Seattle: Parenting Press, 1982-83.

Crary, Elizabeth. *Kids Can Cooperate: A Practical Guide to Teaching Problem Solving*. Seattle: Parenting Press, 1984.

Fry-Miller, Kathleen, and Myers-Walls, Judith. *Young Peacemakers Project Book*. Elgin, Ill.: Brethren Press, 1988.

Haessly, Jacqueline. *Peacemaking: Family Activities for Justice and Peace*. New York: Paulist Press, 1980.

Judson, Stephanie, ed. *A Manual on Nonviolence and Children*. Philadelphia: New Society Publishers, 1977.

Loescher, Elizabeth. *How to Avoid World War III at Home*. Denver, Colo.: The Conflict Center, 1986.

McGinnis, James. *Educating for Peace and Justice: Religious Dimensions, Grades K-6*. St. Louis: Institute for Peace and Justice, 1993.

McGinnis, James. *Educating for Peace and Justice: Religious Dimensions, Grades 7-12*. St. Louis: Institute for Peace and Justice, 1993.

McGinnis, James. *Helping Families Care: Practical Ideas for Intergenerational Programs*. Bloomington, Ind.: Meyer-Stone Books, 1989.

McGinnis, James. *Helping Teens Care*. New York: Crossroad Publishing Company, 1991.

McGinnis, Kathleen. *Dreaming God's Dream: Family Activities Guide, Celebrating the Life and Legacy of Martin Luther King, Jr.* Memphis, Tenn.: Baptist Peace Fellowship of North America, 1989.

McGinnis, Kathleen, and McGinnis, James. *Parenting for Peace and Justice: Ten Years Later*. Maryknoll, N.Y.: Orbis Books, 1990.

McGinnis, Kathleen, and Oehlberg, Barbara. *Starting Out Right: Nurturing Young Children as Peacemakers*. Oak Park, Ill.: Meyer-Stone Books, 1988.

Sehested, Ken, ed. *Dreaming God's Dream: Study Materials for Church, Home and School: Learning-based Activities for Six Age Groups*. Memphis, Tenn.: Baptist Peace Fellowship of North America, 1989.

Trichel, Madeleine Glynn, and Davis, Jo Dee. *A Guide for Teaching Peacemaking*. Columbus, Ohio: The Interfaith Center for Peace, 1988.

Vogt, Susan, ed. *Just Family Nights: 60 Activities to Keep Your Family Together in a World Falling Apart*. Elgin, Ill.: Brethren Press, 1994.

Wichert, Susanne. *Keeping the Peace: Practicing Cooperation and Conflict Resolution with Preschoolers*. Philadelphia: New Society Publishers, 1989.

For Children
Picture Books

Bauld, Jane Scoggins. *Rights for Children*. Austin, Tex.: Futura Communications, 1994.

Buntin, Eve. *The Wall*. New York: Clarion Books, 1990.

Dr. Seuss. *Sneetches and Other Stories*. New York: Random Books, 1961.

Dr. Seuss. *The Butter Battle Book*. New York: Random Books, 1984.

Moore, Joy Hofacker. *Ted Studebaker: A Man Who Loved Peace*. Scottdale, Pa.: Herald Press, 1987.

Pilkey, Dav. *World War Won*. Kansas City, Mo.: Landmark Editions, 1987.

Raschke, Christopher. *R and Я: A Story about Two Alphabets*. Elgin, Ill.: Brethren Press, 1990.

Scholes, Katherine. *Peace Begins with You*. Boston: Little, Brown and Company, 1989.

Tsuchiya, Yukio. *Faithful Elephants: A True Story of Animals, People and War*. Boston: Houghton Mifflin Company, 1988.

Intermediate

Coerr, Eleanor. *Sadako and the Thousand Paper Cranes*. New York: Dell Publishing, 1977.

Eitzen, Ruth. *The White Feather*. Scottdale, Pa.: Herald Press, 1987.

Galicich, Anne. *Samantha Smith: A Journey for Peace*. Minneapolis: Dillon Press, 1987.

Greene, Carol. *Desmond Tutu: Bishop of Peace*. Chicago: Children's Press, 1986.

McKissack, Patricia. *Martin Luther King, Jr.: A Man to Remember*. Chicago: Children's Press, 1984.

Minshull, Evelyn. *The Cornhusk Doll.* Scottdale, Pa.: Herald Press, 1987.

Reynolds, Reginald. *The Truce Story of Gandhi, Man of Peace.* Chicago: Childrens' Press, 1964.

Smith, Samantha. *Journey to the Soviet Union.* Boston: Little, Brown and Co., 1985.

UNICEF. *I Dream of Peace: Images of War by Children of Former Yugoslavia. New York: HarperCollins Publishers, 1994.*

Junior High

Faber, Doris, and Faber, Harold. *Mahatma Gandhi.* New York: Julian Messner, 1986.

Frank, Anne. *The Diary of a Young Church.* New York: Simon & Schuster, 1958.

Harris, Jacqueline. *Martin Luther King, Jr. New York: Franklin Watts, 1983.*

Krauss, Peter. *Sojourner Truth: Antislavery Activist.* New York: Chelsea House Publishers, 1988.

Lehn, Cornelia. *Peace Be With You.* Newton, Kans.: Faith and Life Press, 1980.

Liversidge, Douglas. *Saint Francis of Assisi.* New York: Franklin Watts, 1968.

McKissack, Patricia C., and McKissack, Fredrick. *Sojourner Truth: Ain't I a Woman?* New York: Scholastic, Inc., 1992.

Milne, Teddy. *Kids Who Have Made a Difference.* Northampton, Mass.: Pittenbruach Press, 1989.

Zinkin, Taya. *The Story of Gandhi.* New York: Criterion Books, 1965.